Medallion QUILTS

Inspiration & Patterns

 American Quilter's Society
P. O. Box 3290 • Paducah, KY 42002-3290
www.AmericanQuilter.com

Cindy Vermillion Hamilton

Located in Paducah, Kentucky, the American Quilter's Society (AQS) is dedicated to promoting the accomplishments of today's quilters. Through its publications and events, AQS strives to honor today's quiltmakers and their work and to inspire future creativity and innovation in quiltmaking.

EDITOR: BARBARA SMITH
GRAPHIC DESIGN: ELAINE WILSON
COVER DESIGN: MICHAEL BUCKINGHAM
PHOTOGRAPHY: CHARLES R. LYNCH

Library of Congress Cataloging-in-Publication Data
Hamilton, Cindy Vermillion.
  Medallion quilts: inspiration & patterns / by Cindy Vermillion Hamilton.
    p. cm.
  Summary: "History of medallion quilts with photos from the author's collection. Includes section on designing your own medallion quilt and some patterns"–
Provided by the publisher.
  Includes bibliographical references.
  ISBN 1-57432-907-3
1. Patchwork–Patterns. 2. Quilting–Patterns. I. Title.

TT835.H3348 2006
746.46'041–dc22

                    20066019261

Additional copies of this book may be ordered from the American Quilter's Society, PO Box 3290, Paducah, KY 42002-3290; 800-626-5420 (orders only please); or online at www.AmericanQuilter.com. For all other inquiries, please call 270-898-7903.

CLARISSA'S GARDEN

60" x 60", 1997, hand pieced, hand appliquéd, and hand quilted by the author. The soft, muted fabrics of this medallion are from the Clarissa White Alford Collection, reproduced from an 1886 quilt at the Shelburne Museum in Shelburne, Vermont. The center block, sometimes known as Queen Victoria's Crown or Caesar's Crown, provides the perfect focal point for a medallion design.

Dedication

Dedicated with gratitude to my family for their constant encouragement and love.

Especially to Jessica, Molly, and Robin Wesley, who are the stars in my sky, and to my husband, Ralph, for his unwavering understanding, acceptance, and support.

Also, to my mother, Eleanor Hall Vermillion (1924–1978), who taught me the stitches so long ago, and to my father, Charles Edward Vermillion, for teaching me by example to fly right and to never give up.

Acknowledgment

With special thanks to Barbara Smith, Executive Book Editor at AQS, for her expertise, valuable suggestions, and gentle guidance in helping to make my dreams for this book come true.

Margo's Medallion of 1840,
94" x 94", 2003, hand pieced,
hand appliquéd, and hand
quilted by the author. Many years
of studying antique British and
American medallion quilts culminate
in this quilt. With the exception
of the small dots and corner floral
motifs, this quilt is entirely hand
pieced, including the curved center
block. Several favorite design ideas
are incorporated, including the
spectacular central sunburst and
clamshell borders. This quilt won
first place in the traditional pieced
professional category at the 2004
AQS show.

   Inspiration for fabric choices
came from Margo Krager's reproductions of French fabrics from her
Dargate sample book, dated about
1830. I named the quilt as a tribute
to Margo, in gratitude to her for the
outstanding efforts she has made
to provide quilters like myself with
authentic reproduction fabrics of
quality. Without the fabrics she has
made available, many of my quilts
could not have been made.

Contents

Falling in Love with Medallions

All of us have probably experienced the odd phenomenon of remembering a particular moment when the world as we knew it shifted a bit and we began to see things in a new light. One such moment happened to me in 1974, when I first saw an image of a medallion quilt. I was struck by the concept of a central medallion, framed by a series of borders. Then I was seized by a strange excitement, and the adrenaline began to flow. Many years later, that wonderful sense of excitement still has a hold on me.

A self-taught quilter since 1967, I had, until that moment, thought that a quilt consisted of one block, repeated many times across the surface, and that it would usually be finished with a simple border. Quilts in patterns like Shoo Fly, Triple Sunflower, Baby Bunting, and Nosegay covered my beds and filled my dreams.

In 1974, color photographs and patterns of quilts were hard to find. The few magazines that existed were real treasures for those quilters of the day who were hungry

NORTHUMBERLAND STAR MEDALLION, 97" x 97", 1974, hand pieced and hand quilted by the author. During the early 1970s, it took real effort to find cotton fabrics in a subdued, aged palette that were suitable for this quilt. Nearly every aged-looking piece I had collected was used in it. I had never seen orange and purple together but loved the effect of those colors when put side by side. I experimented with stripes, cutting them across the width of the fabric, and was delighted that they created the effect of many small pieces sewn together.

This quilt taught me that precise marking and stitching were necessary to fit a border of many pieces to a print border. The first time I pieced a strip of Flying Geese, it was about six inches too long, and I had to go back and resew the entire strip.

for patterns, history, and stories about quilts. In one of the magazines, a medallion quilt from Pennsylvania, circa 1820, captured my heart. It consisted of a simple central Eight-Pointed Star block, surrounded by borders of more stars, triangles, and pinwheels.

Immediately, I set to work, searching my growing, treasured fabric stash for prints in aged tones and colors similar to those in that quilt. Not wanting to copy it, I created my own medallion design by enlarging a traditional Northumberland Star block for the center then building several borders to surround it. As with every quilt since then, this one taught me many lessons about using fabric to best advantage, how to draft my own patterns for blocks and borders, and most importantly, how to make all those borders fit. When this quilt, NORTHUMBERLAND STAR MEDALLION, was exhibited at the Archuleta County Fair and the Colorado State Fair, it was enthusiastically received, despite being considered a very odd design. Most quilters of the day were unaware of the medallion quilt style.

Designing and sewing medallion quilts never gets tedious or boring for me. Because the design process proceeds as the stitching progresses, I never know what the finished quilt will look like until the last border is in place. I begin with the central image, but after that, the quilt speaks to me and lets me know what should come

NORTHUMBERLAND STAR MEDALLION (detail of the center) hand pieced and hand quilted by the author

next. Then comes a rather fuzzy image in my mind, a foggy sketch on paper, and an approximate finished size. Next, I select a pile of possible fabrics and draft the center pattern. At this point, I have only a faint idea about where the design will lead. Perhaps I want to have a border of a certain pieced or appliquéd design, or cut from a special border fabric. These borders will come into focus more clearly as the quilt progresses. Working in this spontaneous, creative manner keeps my interest and energy running at an obsessively high level. It is impossible for me to stop working on a medallion top once it is underway. Because of this, I have never left a quilt in this design style unfinished.

Now, more than thirty years and fifty medallion quilts later, I continue to make quilts in other styles, but the medallion design is the one I return to again and again. Inspiration for a new medallion quilt comes from many different sources and always hits like a lightning bolt. Some of the quilts began as a desire to memorialize a particular place, time, or event. A feeling of love or patriotism can inspire a medallion. A desire to closely replicate a particular historical period can provide ideas for both the design of the top as well as the quilting. In addition, the numerous magnificent reproduction and novelty fabrics that are available today are incredibly inspiring.

In this age of speed techniques and "quick and easy" quiltmaking, I sometimes feel like an anachronism. Most of the piecing in these quilts is done by hand, as are the appliqué and quilting stitches. Always, my goal is to create a functional, authentic quilt that looks beautiful from across a room as well as up close, as if viewed on a bed. I want my quilt to look like a quilt rather than a painting. I strive for a "patina" that only hand quilting can give, meaning a surface with nostalgic and tactile appeal that has been created, with much use and work, by the human hand. When working with a historical design idea and using reproduction fabrics, I like to imagine that a woman from that era would recognize my quilt as something familiar to her, a quilt that might have been created during her lifetime. Authenticity in design, fabric selection, and construction techniques are all extremely important to me.

Whether you choose to sew by hand or machine, you can create a beautiful quilt by closely following the patterns given here, or you can use a pattern as a starting place, making changes as your quilt progresses. It may simply be a matter of changing a border pattern or two to ones you like better, or substituting a different design for the center block. The design choices and methods for making these patterns are truly limitless.

It is my hope that, by sharing these patterns and quilts, quiltmakers everywhere will also be struck by the wonder of this design style that provides so many avenues for creative expression. With great joy, I present this collection of favorite patterns and photographs of medallion quilts I have stitched and loved— quilts that literally have been the threads of my life.

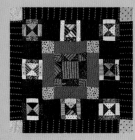

Pieces of History

As a teenager, I was swept away by the world of quiltmaking because it held everything I was passionate about: the history of women and the world, along with art and craft. Quilts are my magic carpets, carrying me to places of the past, filled with secrets.

How fascinating it is to realize that the design of each medallion quilt we sew today can be traced back to the first trading ships on the high seas, possibly even to a ship that was returning to Portugal after stopping at ports in India. A British merchant ship captured this vessel in 1592, and the spoils were taken to England to be sold. Deep within the hold of the ship was a cargo of strange, wonderful cotton fabrics that were block printed or hand painted with bright patterns of exotic flowering vines, trees, and strange animals.

Garments of domestically manufactured wool and linen had clothed the people of Europe for centuries. At one point, it became illegal in England and France to wear Indian cottons because of the

threat to domestic wool and linen production, but desire for the washable, colorful cotton fabrics from India quickly grew among the wealthy folks of Europe, who could afford the expensive imports.

From reports of European traders about 1600, we know that there were two main types of cotton prints produced in India. The first was an allover pattern of flowering vines, which we now call "chintz." The second was a printed spread known as a "palampore" or bed cover. At the center of the design was a large tree, growing from decorative hillocks at its base and sprouting exotic flowers and fruits. This central design was surrounded by one or more decorative borders of floral or paisley motifs. Sometimes these textiles were shipped from India as a piece of fabric to be finished later, and others were shipped as quilted bed coverings.

The early palampores were eagerly purchased by wealthy Europeans, who soon decorated bedchambers with the delightful, washable cotton fabrics from India. The look of a bedspread that had a central design that fit the top of the bed and borders that dropped down the sides became engraved in the women's minds. Colonists in America brought this idea with them in their quilts and their minds, and as the new country began, medallion quilts similar to those made in Europe adorned the beds of the more affluent immigrants. This design convention has been used repeatedly throughout the centuries, and it is still with us today, four hundred years later.

At first, drawing heavily on English ideas of "frame" quilts, as they were known across the Atlantic, women in America eventually developed their own styles of medallion quilts, such as a Star of Bethlehem framed by borders. Simple border blocks, used in English framed medallions, were repeated and modified in America, where development of star patterns, such as Sawtooth, Variable Star, and Eight-Pointed Star became increasingly popular.

By 1850, the idea of block-style quilts, set with sashing and small corner blocks, was in full bloom in America, and for many, the medallion quilt style seemed old-fashioned. However, existing antique quilts from the last half of the 1800s provide evidence that women continued to make medallion quilts, no matter what other styles were in vogue.

With the availability of reproduction fabrics from all time periods, including reproductions of those first imports of 1592, today's quiltmakers have an incredible abundance of prints to make into beautiful medallion quilts. We have large-scale toiles and chintzes for centers, stripes for borders, and an amazing number of possibilities for block and border designs.

More than four hundred years of images from textiles and quilts in books and museums inspire and delight us. With medallion quilts as our magic carpets, we can go wherever we want in time. We can sew our stories into our quilts, leaving tales of our time in the stitches for those who come after us, just as women have always done.

Gems from the Author's Collection

WHIG ROSE MEDALLION, ca. 1850, 96" x 97", collection of the author. Here is an example of typical patterns and fabrics that were popular during the mid 1800s, when the style known as "red and green" was most popular. The medallion format in this quilt, however, is unusual for red and green quilts, which were usually block or album style, with squares of identical size making up the top. This quiltmaker seems to be using a design format that was becoming old-fashioned, while working with the newest turkey red fabrics and popular patterns of her time.

CAMPBELL FAMILY SUNBURST, ca. 1860, 88" x 96", collection of the author. Hand stitched by a member of the Campbell family from western Pennsylvania, this quilt is an outstanding example of folk-art design. The quiltmaker includes celestial and floral motifs and a central medallion that emphasizes the sun. Note that miniature versions of the center square are repeated in the middle border of blocks.

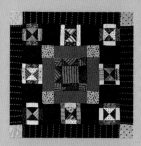

TWO-SIDED BRITISH MEDALLION, ca. 1895, 73" x 87", Great Britain, collection of the author. Here is a classic example of the pieced medallion-style quilts made in the British Isles as late as the turn of the nineteenth century. The design is little changed from quilts pieced one hundred years earlier. Only the fabrics are different. Typical of quilts from the United Kingdom, it is hand quilted in an overall wave design and finished in the knife-edge style, in which the front and back are turned toward each other and a line of stitching closes the outer edge. Two different medallion tops were quilted together, creating an unusual two-sided quilt.

LEFT: **BUTTERFLIES AND BOWTIES MEDALLION,** ca. 1935, 80" x 88", Virginia, collection of the author. While many fancy, appliquéd medallion quilts were made during the early twentieth-century quilt revival, it is rare to find a pieced medallion from this time period. Clearly, the maker spent many moments of pleasure working with the light, cheerful colors and prints of the 1930s as she stitched her favorite blocks into a medallion. Hopefully, the time spent creating her masterpiece helped keep the woes of the Great Depression far away.

RIGHT: **SAWTOOTH STAR MEDALLION,** ca. 1890, 79"x 84", collection of the author. Made in a favorite color scheme for the time, this pink and brown quilt was sewn by a quiltmaker in Pennsylvania. At the time, the medallion format was very old-fashioned. The three outer borders of prints, which date from a later period, must have been added several years after the interior section was completed. Note how the maker repeated three hourglass blocks from the center, using them as corners in the sawtooth border.

TRADITIONAL ENGLISH MEDALLION, ca. 1870, 91" x 96", Great Britain, collection of the author. The central rosette is surrounded by hexagons whose sides measure 1¼". The center is pieced by the English method of basting patches over hexagon-shaped paper templates then joining the hexagons with a whipstitch. A border of half-square triangles follows, pieced from a wonderful variety of cotton prints. Like many other quilts made in the United Kingdom at this time, Perkin's purple is prominent in the color scheme. We know that Queen Victoria herself was caught up in the rage for fabrics colored with this then-new synthetic dye. Two rows of elongated hexagons form the next border, in a pattern known in England as "Church Windows." Borders of rectangles, then squares, and finally a 9½" wide print border beautifully finish this traditional medallion.

ANTIQUE ENGLISH MEDALLION, ca. 1890, 83" x 88", collection of the author. This medallion of many pieces from England has at its center five miniature 3" blocks. The borders include pieced patterns typically seen in English frame quilts throughout the nineteenth century, such as Squares-on-Point, Brickwork, Zigzag, and Flying Geese. Very unusual for a quilt of this origin and style is the 1½" folded triangle outer edge, widely known today as "prairie points."

Selecting Fabric

From the beginning of my involvement with quiltmaking, my goal was to produce a quilt that could be identified with a particular time period. By studying antique quilts in museums and books, I developed a feel for fabrics and colors that have appeared in quilts throughout history. Fabrics from general time periods go together well and look right together. Quiltmakers of the 1930s used solids and whites, for example, to unify and provide stability when working with the riot of color found in the prints of the day. In the early 1800s, a cream or white solid was sometimes used to add stability and sparkle to quilts made from large floral chintzes. Fabric designers of today make it easier than ever for quilters to choose prints that work together harmoniously. We have access to wonderful collections of prints in a variety of scales and types, specifically designed to work well with each other.

SUNRISE IN MY GARDEN, 52" x 52", 2005, hand pieced and hand quilted by the author. Most of the fabrics in this quilt are from Xenia Cord's Bannister Hall collection.

A beautiful morning sunrise in a tranquil English garden is captured in this classic medallion design. My goal was to stitch a quilt that could have been created in the early 1800s, the period during which the original fabrics that inspired these exciting reproductions were first printed.

This quilt is an example of how a printed stripe can add intricacy and interest to the petals of the sunburst without the quiltmaker having to stitch extra pieces. Simple, basic borders commonly seen in antique English medallions fill out the design. To add to the authenticity of the technique and design, the outer border incorporates a traditional English quilting pattern known in the British Isles as the "Weardale Chain."

For a no-fail starting point, select a few fabrics from one designer's collection, such as a geometric print and a floral print that are just dynamite when placed together. Even if you select several prints from a collection, add others of your own choosing to avoid over-coordinating or matching the fabrics. Remember, you don't have to coordinate fabrics as if you were going to wear them! Give yourself freedom to play with color any way you want, and don't worry about what other people will think of your choices. Include several surprises in your selection to keep the quilt lively and interesting.

For many quilters, selecting fabrics is one of the most creative, enjoyable parts of making a quilt. One of the challenges I enjoy is using as many different prints as possible. I try to repeat colors and patterns throughout the top, while using variety in scale and type of print, including everything from large-scale paisleys, florals, toiles, and stripes to small geometrics. To avoid boredom and to add sparkle and interest, use several similar prints of a particular color, rather than using the same print over and over. Selecting colors (not necessarily in the same print) that are used in the center and repeating them in the outer sections of the quilt top will help to pull the eye outward and unite the elements in the design.

If quilting design is important to you, include areas of solid fabrics that will show detailed quilting stitches to best advantage. Fine-quality solid white or cream cotton was frequently used in antique quilts, so consider using it if you are reproducing a quilt from the past. Sometimes a solid may be just what is needed to provide a pleasing contrast with busy prints. Remember that solids blend in more with other fabrics after they have been quilted and textured with stitches.

WHERE LIBERTY DWELLS MEDALLION, 85" x 85", 2004, hand pieced, hand appliquéd, and hand quilted by the author. Notice how the fabric colors and patterns are repeated throughout the quilt, and there is considerable variety in the size and type of print.

Inspiration for this medallion came from a desire to use many of the wonderful reproduction fabrics from Brackman and Thompson's Remember the Ladies fabric line. The wide outer border allowed me to use large pieces of the toile depicting George Washington and Benjamin Franklin's apotheosis, or ascent to god-like status. The strange "ball" border appears on a quilt made in North Carolina circa 1815.

Contrast in both color and value is an important consideration when selecting fabrics. Choosing a variety of values results in contrast between light and dark, which helps to create drama and visual interest in your design. I frequently use the lightest fabrics in the center medallion and then choose a slightly darker shade for each subsequent border, so the darkest fabrics are at the outside edges of the quilt. This seems to help draw the eye to the center. Keep in mind the idea of framing a picture. The fabrics and colors in the borders should frame the central design and enhance it, without drawing too much attention away from the center.

Occasionally, I use a light fabric in the center and then over-dye it with a beige shade to be used in the outer borders, helping to create a subtle center focus. If possible, check the contrast of the work in progress by viewing it in a variety of light conditions, from dim to very bright. A dimly lit room will immediately reveal whether or not the contrast in your fabrics works the way you want.

In addition to contrast in value, special attention should be paid to the selection and use of contrasting colors, those that appear opposite each other on the color wheel. For example, adding just a hint of orange or rust to a quilt that contains a lot of blue can be the spice that wakes everything up and starts your colors dancing. You don't need to use a color wheel. Just experiment by adding other colors to what you have already selected. Keep trying different values and colors until your fabrics start to dance. If you are in doubt about your choices, continue to audition different color ideas until the quilt looks great to you. No one needs to tell you when this happens. You will intuitively know.

If your selection looks blah, you may need more contrast in color, value, or both. Remember, you can increase interest and variety by adding any number of

COLUMBUS MEDALLION,

99" x 99", 1992, hand pieced, hand appliquéd, reverse appliquéd, hand embroidered, and hand quilted by the author. The solid blue triangles in the pieced border accent the blue in the center block and bring the quilt to life. Jinny Beyer's wonderful 1992 Discovery fabric collection was the inspiration for this medallion. The central Mariner's Compass motif was the perfect place for my carefully researched appliquéd ship. The fascinating toile includes vignettes that range from the early days of Columbus' voyage to the New World, to the Statue of Liberty, and the space shuttle.

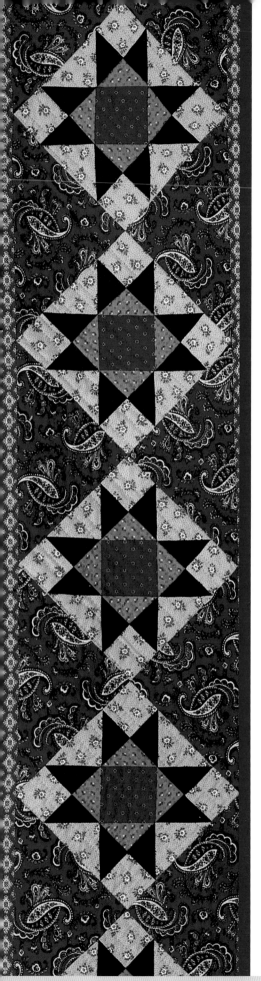

RED BARN MEDALLION, 86" x 86", 1983, hand pieced, hand appliquéd and hand quilted by the author. The center started out with medium values, and I didn't realize that the border fabrics couldn't be any lighter than what I had already used in the center, because the eye would be drawn away from the central focus. The quilt, therefore, ended up darker than I had originally envisioned. The lesson learned was to use the brightest, lightest colors in the center.

This quilt is a tribute in cloth to the huge old barn my first husband and I salvaged and moved to the family ranch in 1976. Originally located at the foot of Wolf Creek Pass, the structure was a local landmark and had appeared in calendars and jigsaw puzzles. We were thrilled to be able to save it from demolition.

neutral prints, no matter what color scheme you have chosen. Keep in mind that sparing use of a contrasting color can turn an ordinary quilt into something spectacular.

When auditioning fabrics for your quilt, it is wise to view them from a distance. A reducing glass is useful for this purpose. Sometimes diagonal lines or patterns that jump out from a distance are not evident when viewed close up. Colors may pop out and the fabric may appear very different from what you see from just a few inches away. Now is the time to be aware of these effects. Be sure to note major repeats of figures in large-scale prints and plan for the placement of these repeats.

When choosing fabrics for a border, pay careful attention to the contrast between adjoining sections, making sure the next border shows clearly against what has come before. To view your choices, arrange the fabrics on a table or the floor, folding them to a size that approximates the amount that will be used in each border. If possible, leave the fabrics laid out for several days, looking at them each time you pass by. View them close up, from a distance, and through a reducing glass. Note how differences occur as lighting changes. Never make major decisions about fabric choices when you are tired or in a hurry. These important decisions need to be made when you are at your best and your mind is fresh.

When you have selected and planned fabrics for a border, cut just a few pieces and lay them out to determine if they work the way you have envisioned. To avoid frustration and wasted time and fabric, never cut all the fabrics for the border strips until you are positive they will work well and give the desired effect. Patience during this time of planning, along with a willingness to let the quilt speak to you as choices are made, will pay off in a quilt you can be proud of, and you will know that you have truly done your best.

TEMPUS FUGIT (TIME FLIES), 87" x 98", 2000, hand pieced, hand appliquéd, reverse appliquéd, and hand quilted by the author. The touches of orange are the perfect counterpoint for this predominantly blue quilt.

The center design of TEMPUS FUGIT was inspired by a magnificent floor mosaic in the Basilica di San Marco, in Venice, Italy. This quilt traveled the world with other finalists in the Houston International Quilt Festival's exhibit of millennium quilts, entitled "A quilt for the year 2000."

Quilters know and understand the meaning of time especially well because time is the necessary element that is needed to produce works of great beauty and deeply personal meaning. To a quilter, every moment counts. Like our quilts, life itself is a patchwork of minutes, stitched together into a piece of time that we call a life or a millennium.

Making Borders Fit

Cutting and piecing borders that fit is the biggest challenge when sewing a medallion quilt. Measuring correctly is critical. Quilts always seem to grow and spread out along the edges. Each time you add a border, you'll want to be aware of this and take steps to keep your quilt top square. By measuring the length and width of your quilt top through the center when planning each border, you can prevent spreading. Making every effort to conform to the quilt measurements each time a border is added will help to create a quilt top that has square corners and lies flat.

It is advisable to cut and sew no more than one half of a pieced border strip before trying it on for fit. If it is too large or too small at this point, adjustments can be made in the seam allowances for a better fit. It is important to understand that adding even a pencil width to a seam allowance when joining a long strip of border units can quickly make a border too long. The first medallion top I made taught me this. Remember that, if you add even one-sixteenth inch to each unit of sixteen flying geese, you will have added an extra inch by the time all the geese are joined in a strip.

When you have sewn one-fourth to one-half of a border, it is time for an evaluation of the fabrics. Are the colors and contrast working as you envisioned? Is the border going to fit the quilt top without having to stretch it or gather it in? Do you need to change something? If you are not pleased with how the border works, this is the time to make changes. If you leave something in the quilt top that you really don't like, your eye will always be drawn to it first, and it will bother you. It is worth the extra time and wasted fabric to create a quilt you will love in the end.

In summary, if you can create an interesting center, the rest will follow. Plan carefully before you cut and sew, and stand back often to review what you've stitched at a distance. Accept that your quilt will not be perfect. There is probably no such thing as a perfect quilt. Whether you sew by hand, machine, or a combination of both, medallion quilts provide the perfect canvas for personal expression.

Striped Borders

Striped borders can add pizzazz to your quilt. When cutting printed stripes, determine the center of the stripe (across its width) then immediately cut the other three border strips, so that they are identical.

TEMPUS FUGIT

MAKE MUCH OF TIME

Ten Reasons to Sew by Hand

Of course, your medallion quilt can be made by machine, but there are a number of advantages to hand piecing:

1. Hand stitching can be done anywhere at almost any time, which provides an opportunity to use up little pieces of time as well as fabric. I always have a project close at hand, ready to pick up when the opportunity arises. I mark pieces for stitching while doing other things, such as talking on the telephone, and I always carry a few blocks to work on when I go somewhere or have a few free moments to sew.

2. Hand piecing makes it possible to piece more difficult patterns, such as those with curved pieces or inset seams, with more precise results (and for me, less frustration) than I can get on the sewing machine. This technique allows me to piece any pattern I want, whereas the sewing machine limits my design choices.

3. I find hand stitching enjoyable, relaxing, and more comfortable because I can sit in my favorite chair with my feet propped up, and I can stitch anywhere, including places like out on the porch or at the park in the summertime. As an analogy, would you rather read a book on the computer or lying down somewhere really comfortable?

4. Hand sewing provides a quiet little oasis where it is possible to find peace, tranquility, and relaxation. It can take you to a place away from the distractions and stresses of modern life. In this place, you can step out of the rat race and put things into perspective. For me, it's like meditation. You can't hurry it up, speed it up, or rush through it. You have to take one stitch at a time, and I find this gentle activity to be amazingly calming and refreshing.

5. If you want, hand stitching enables you to step back into history. The authenticity of the technique allows you to identify closely with women of the eighteenth and nineteenth centuries, before the sewing machine was found in most households. You can create reproductions that are very close to antique quilts. At the same time, you are recreating a similar experience and activity in which women of another time and place participated. I enjoy creating authentic quilts that could be placed in a particular time period, and the people of that time and place wouldn't notice anything strange about them. My quilt would seem totally contemporary with their culture and experience. Authenticity in material and technique is important to me.

6. Hand sewing allows a quilter to develop intimate connections with fabrics because she can look at them longer, touching and manipulating them over and over, rather than stacking, cutting, and running them through a machine. You have time and opportunity to really see and appreciate their beauty, colors, patterns, and designs, as well as to experience the pleasure of touching and feeling the fabrics.

7. Working with templates means you don't have to read a lot of directions and cutting measurements. It is a good technique for right-brained, visually oriented people who don't enjoy working through long lists of numbers and fractions.

8. A hand-stitched quilt has softness and a patina to it that is different from a machine-pieced quilt. There is an intangible but very real spirit that resides in a quilt that has been made by hand. It is as though the maker's handwritten signature covers every square inch.

9. Hand quilting skills improve as you become more adept at wearing a thimble and piecing by hand. Finger strength, skill, and dexterity grow as you hand piece, which can improve your hand-quilting stitches.

10. Finally, I choose not to rush through time. I want to capture and hold time and slow it down. That's one of the biggest reasons why I make quilts. Hand sewing allows me to step out of time and let it go. I can enjoy and savor the journey as much as or more than getting to the destination. A quilt is a time capsule—a statement of its time and the person who made it. To me, quilts, especially those made by hand, are mystical, spiritual objects that contain stories of a unique time and place hidden in the stitches.

Designing Your Own Medallion

After making a medallion quilt or two from the patterns on pages 57–124, you may want to try your hand at making a quilt of your very own design. When it comes to designing and sewing medallion quilts, there are just two rules to follow: (1) There are no rules. (2) You need to be flexible, that is, able to change and adapt your ideas at any stage. If you can follow these "rules," you will find making medallion quilts to be an exciting, creative, fascinating adventure at all stages of construction. My intention here is to share with you some of the techniques and procedures that consistently work for me. Use them as suggestions or as starting points for developing your own ideas. As your experience and confidence grow, you will discover your own favorite techniques for designing and constructing your quilts.

Keep in mind that, in creating a medallion quilt, you can let go of the idea that every piece and color has to be mapped out carefully before taking a single stitch. Remember also that making a one-of-a-kind quilt by hand or machine produces an object that is different in quality from a factory-made, mass-produced item. Little imperfections in stitching and construction are perfectly acceptable and even desirable when it comes to quiltmaking. Here's a little secret: I never made a perfect quilt, and I'm sure I never will!

Finding Design Ideas

The most important thing when designing a medallion quilt is simply to start the process. The starting point can be a dearly loved pieced or appliquéd quilt block, a photograph of an antique quilt that captivates your imagination, or some special fabrics that work together beautifully. Once this starting

MORNING SONG MEDALLION, 100" x 100", 1995, hand and machine pieced, hand appliquéd, and hand quilted by the author. This quilt echoes design conventions of traditional English frame quilts. Many of the fabrics used in it were reproduced in Great Britain from 1800s' quilts found there. Bird, flower, and nest motifs, like those in this quilt, are seen in British quilts of that time. In America, we see them first in printed chintz fabrics from the early 1800s as well as in some indigo on white appliquéd medallion quilts. Later, about 1850, these motifs appear in profusion in red and green appliqué quilts, such as the famous Baltimore Album masterpieces. The sawtooth border framing the central oval and the Steeplechase blocks can be found on quilts of Welsh and English origin.

Wide outer borders provide the perfect place to use today's reproduction fabrics, such as large-scale toile, chintz, and pillar prints. Many of today's reproduction fabric lines include both large- and medium-scale chintzes that work well together, providing an excellent starting place for selecting fabrics. A foolproof method for choosing fabrics is to purchase the border prints first and then select scraps or fat quarters that blend in color and time period with the border prints.

A Quilter's Voice, 98" x 98", 1995, hand pieced, hand appliquéd, and hand quilted by the author. In the early 1990s, fabric manufacturers started making fabric collections reproduced from quilts in museums. The first museum was the Smithsonian Institution, which authorized RJR Fashion Fabrics to create a collection based on Mary Totten's Rising Sun quilt, pieced about 1830. I chose to use the fabrics in this classic medallion quilt as a way to showcase the magnificent prints, particularly the toiles and the large-scale chintz in the border. This quilt won first place in Salute to Quiltmakers of the Past, a contest sponsored by Quilter's Newsletter Magazine and RJR Fashion Fabrics. The quilt appeared on the magazine cover in November 1995.

place is in focus, you are on your way to creating a medallion quilt. At this point, it is time to spend several nights, while going to sleep, imagining the endless design possibilities for this quilt that is about to be born.

Here are some possible design strategies. Sometimes, one exceptionally beautiful border-stripe fabric sets the mood and colors for the design that follows. MORNING SONG MEDALLION began this way. The oval central appliqué design evolved from the floral stripe and the ovals in the outer border fabric. A QUILTER'S VOICE, page 32, began with the outer border of the spectacular, large chintz floral fabric, in addition to a desire to commemorate the work of quiltmakers from long ago.

Sometimes your design might begin with a collection of fabrics developed around a theme, such as a favorite garden, a current or historical event, a special pet, an admired person, or a feeling such as patriotism, love, or friendship. FRISKEY'S GARDEN (pattern begins on page 94) grew out of a desire to capture the colors, sounds, and smells of one August morning as I walked through fields of sunflowers, accompanied by a dear feline friend.

CRAZY ANNE'S FANCY (pattern begins on page 82) was designed around a beautiful collection of fabrics reproduced from quilts in the American Textile History Museum in Lowell, Massachusetts. This quilt honors the young girls and women who labored long hours in the textile mills to produce the beautiful fabrics of the nineteenth century, similar to those used in this quilt.

Another major source of design inspiration can come from a desire to make a quilt that represents a particular period in history. Carefully studying antique quilts at museums, exhibits, or in books and magazines can provide direction and motivation to begin a medallion quilt. If an intricate block-

style quilt captures your heart, consider enlarging just one block to use as a medallion center. Design borders to enhance this one special block, repeating elements from the block.

Pay attention to quilts that catch your attention and ask yourself why you are drawn to them. Take some time with a quilt you love to thoroughly analyze why it appeals to you so much. Is it the color? Pattern? Fabric? Does it just have soul that reaches out and touches you? A message from a quiltmaker of long ago?

LEFT. **Journey of Lewis and Clark,** 96" x 96", 2005, hand pieced and hand quilted by the author. Notice how starting with a diamond center impacts the design. Made with dramatic fabrics designed to commemorate the Corps of Discovery's 1804 journey, this quilt combines Native American motifs, American eagles, and patterns of movement that subtly express the spirit of the great expedition.

The center star block represents Native American beadwork patterns. The American eagle reminds me of President Jefferson's push to explore new territories. Brackman and Thompson's wonderful toile depicting major participants in the expedition provides the perfect ground for the center star.

Sketching Your Quilt

Most medallion quilts are designed around a center that covers roughly one-fourth to one-third of the quilt. For example, if you are planning a large quilt about 90" square, the center would measure between 22" and 30". I usually use about 25" for a center starting measurement. This allows for the addition of strips or borders but keeps the top from ending up too large.

You can start designing with a vague, overall idea of the look and feel of the quilt center. The borders can come into focus later. On a piece of paper, make a pencil sketch, determining the shape of the center block. Instead of a square, you might select to use a circle, oval, octagon, or hexagon. If you choose a square, decide whether it will be left as a square, as frequently seen in British frame quilts, or turned on point, creating a diamond. Turning the block on point creates four large triangles that provide a perfect canvas for appliqué or piecing or a large-scale print, which can complement and enhance the center.

Planning Pieced Borders

I don't usually draft patterns for borders until I have stitched the central part of the medallion. With the center completed, I have an actual piece to determine accurate measurements, and the next section of the quilt will start to come into focus. I decide on a border design, and at this point, I use graph paper for drafting pattern pieces, and a calculator to determine the number and size of the units that will fit along the previously attached border. Keep in mind that an odd number of repeats allows you to center a motif in the border, so that the ends of the border strips will be identical. This arrangement may be helpful when placing colors or patterns so that border strips are symmetrical and balanced.

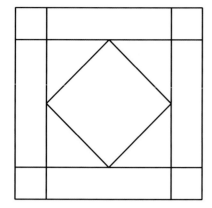

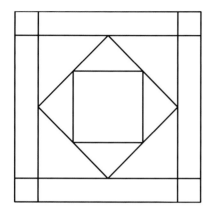

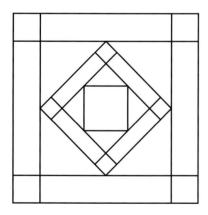

Diamond in a Square. Simple grids such as these can be the starting points for designing medallion quilts.

Frequently, a design can start with an underlying grid, such as a Diamond-in-a-Square Amish quilt pattern. Think of the spaces in these patterns as areas to be filled with patchwork, appliqué, or quilting designs, or you can use sections of a large-scale fabric you love in these spaces.

If you are designing your quilt around a special stripe or border fabric, areas for this are sketched in at this time, and measurements for the width of these strips are noted. Perhaps you want to use a large-scale toile de Jouy as a dramatic, wide outer border. You will probably want to use this same fabric somewhere in the interior of the quilt, and this is a good time to plan another place where it can be used.

Your pencil sketch can show a general idea of the size of the center block, the finished quilt, and perhaps the width of some of the borders. Keep in mind that, most of the time, borders increase in size toward the edges of the quilt, and there is frequently more detail in design toward the center.

As you begin to lay out possible fabrics, the idea for the center will come into sharper focus, and you can begin to draft and draw details of patterns to be used. At this point, you may sketch in some corner blocks, but always reserve the right to change your mind later. Whether your corner blocks are pieced, appliquéd, or fabric squares, reserve final decisions until the border is stitched and you are ready to sew it to the quilt.

Corner blocks are important parts of medallion quilt design. These areas can repeat and reinforce portions of the center design. They can emphasize colors or fabrics already used, or introduce fabrics that will be used in other borders. Corners can be used to add weight to a design and to give the eye a resting place, in the way a period ends a sentence and prepares us for the next idea. Corner blocks can relate to other sections with color, fabric, or pattern, providing a pathway that carries the eye from the center outward and back again.

Sketch of Hamilton Wedding
Quilt. This rough sketch of the Hamilton Wedding Quilt is an example of how I begin most medallion quilts. Compare this sketch with the photo of the quilt. I don't use graph paper until it is time to draft the center, corner blocks, and borders.

Hamilton Wedding Quilt

Hamilton Wedding Quilt, 89" x 89", 1994, hand pieced, hand appliquéd and hand quilted by the author. Living in southwest Colorado makes one very aware and interested in the cultures of Native Americans. My husband and I spent many days exploring the ruins of ancient Pueblo peoples and learning about nearby Navajo and Ute tribes.

Made to celebrate our wedding, this quilt incorporates some Native American designs that are similar to those used by quilters of European descent. Sunburst designs like that in the center can be found painted on hide robes and dwellings and carved into stone as petroglyphs. Floral designs, such as those in the corners of the center, appear in beadwork of the Northeastern tribes. Animal totems like the snake and the deer are believed to guide individuals on their life's journey, providing wisdom and protection.

One of the many fabrics with Southwestern themes printed during the 1990s was utilized for the triangular design print borders. This striking fabric inspired the design and color choices for this quilt.

How Much Fabric Should I Buy?

Suggested yardage is given with each pattern, but the following information and table can help you determine the yardage requirements for medallions of your own design.

When figuring the yardage for print borders for a large quilt approximately 100" square, keep in mind that 3 yards of fabric yields four lengthwise border strips that measure 10" x 108".

To estimate the length of bias you will need when cutting strips for an appliquéd border vine, lay a piece of string along one border strip, following the curve you will use for the vine. Measure the length of the string, multiply by 4, and add a foot or two to the length so you will have plenty. Multiply this length by the cut width of one of the bias strips to find the area (square inches) of the fabric piece needed. Take the square root of this number to find the size of the square you will need for cutting the strips. Add a couple of inches to the square for good measure then divide this measurement by 36" to find the yardage.

yards	location
3½	Large-scale borders 8"–10" wide. Allows for cutting motifs the same on all four borders.
2⅝	Inner borders, such as stripes. This will give you lengths of 90" that you will not have to piece.
2–4	Subtle background for center medallion with fabric to repeat in the borders.
½–1	Use for a major statement in several areas. One yard can make a definite statement in a quilt. If you run out, you can fill in with a similar fabric.
¼–½ each	A variety of prints for corners and pieced borders, as well as a fabric or two to use sparingly as an accent to spice things up.
1	For binding (allows some extra)
9	Backing (allows for 3 panels 108" long)

Made with Love by the Author

Gathered here for your inspiration and enjoyment is a selection of many of the medallion quilts I have made. Most of them are hand pieced. All appliqué and quilting was done by hand.

I approach quiltmaking by trying my best to plan and stitch design elements that enhance and enrich each area of the surface. The soul of a quilt, for me, comes shining through, especially in the colors and the quilting stitches. These are the aspects that reach out and grab my interest and my heart. For me, these are the elements that make the difference between a good quilt and one that becomes emblazoned in my memory.

By sharing these works of my heart and soul with you, I hope to encourage and inspire quilters who desire to make their own magnificent medallions. Enjoy!

Olde English Medallion,
104" x 104", 1992, hand pieced, hand appliquéd, and hand quilted. Images of medallion quilts from the British Isles inspired the design and colors in this medallion quilt, which is in the permanent collection of the Museum of the American Quilter's Society. It was thrilling to win first place in Traditional Pieced Professional at the Paducah show in 1992. This quilt appeared in the AQS wall calendar and on the cover of *Quilter's Newsletter Magazine* in November 1993.

My Fair Quilt, 95" x 95", 2001, hand pieced, hand appliquéd, and hand quilted. In 1974, a dream came true when I moved to Pagosa Springs, Colorado. One of the first things I did was to enter a recently finished quilt in the Archuleta County Fair. What a thrill it was to win a blue ribbon for my Triple Sunflower quilt. I was hooked on the challenge and excitement of competitions.

MY FAIR QUILT recalls happy, heat-filled, dusty August days at the county fair. It is a collage of animals, feed sacks, flowers, grain and feed crops, and the wonderful needlework and quilts we still see at our state and county fairs. It is a celebration of fairs of the past, present, and future where men, women, and children of all ages have a chance to show off their best efforts, share them with others, and maybe even bring home a coveted blue ribbon!

Halley's Comet Medallion, 84" x 84", 1986, hand pieced, hand appliquéd, and hand quilted. A vivid childhood memory is that of sitting in my classroom around 1955, listening to the teacher tell about a spectacular comet that would be visible from earth in the far away year of 1986. I promised myself I would be there to see it. I roused my sleepy family from their beds one night about 2:30 a.m., and we stood outside, shivering in the cold mountain air, marveling at the smudge in the sky that was Halley's comet.

The design for the comet in the center of this quilt was inspired by a stamp issued by the British Philatelic Bureau on February 18,1986. The stamp featured a woodblock print of the comet as seen in an ancient text. This quilt is also a memorial to the crew of the Challenger, who so tragically lost their lives in 1986.

Liberty's Centennial Medallion, *72" x 72", 1986, hand pieced, hand appliquéd, reverse appliquéd, and hand quilted.* By the year 1986, the Statue of Liberty was one hundred years old. Sadly neglected and in need of repair, the statue was the focus of much publicity during the early 1980s. A campaign was launched to collect the huge sums of money needed to repair and refurbish Lady Liberty so that she could survive into the next century.

A contest was held by the Museum of American Folk Art (MAFA) to honor the statue. This quilt provided the perfect opportunity to stitch the eagle I had wanted to use in the center of a medallion, and Liberty's crown was the ideal motif to fill the corner triangles. Liberty's Centennial Medallion was selected as Colorado's second place winner in the MAFA contest, and the quilt toured the country in the "Liberties With Liberty" folk-art exhibition, curated by Sandi Fox.

Davis Ranch Medallion, 84" x 84", 1982, hand pieced, hand appliquéd, and hand quilted. When I first saw the delightful child's quilt top on the cover of a book, I knew that someday I would make a similar quilt about my family's home. The central portion of my medallion depicts the log cabin where my children were raised, on the Davis family ranch in Southwestern Colorado. The three stars in the sky represent my children. Red and Dude, favorite horses, and Buckwheat, our golden retriever, are also memorialized. As in real life, the log cabin home is surrounded by the beauty of the delectable San Juan Mountains.

My Heart's Delight Medallion, 100" x 100", 1987, hand pieced, hand appliquéd, and hand quilted. My love for Pennsylvania German motifs and design, patterns that show movement, and exquisite hand quilting all come together in this quilt. Red and green quilts are usually designed in block style, but I wanted to create an unusual medallion format for some of my favorite motifs found on antique quilts. I designed this quilt with a lot of room for beautiful hand-quilted motifs, also inspired by Pennsylvania German design. I think that much of the beauty of this quilt is in the hand-quilted details.

Christmas Medallion, 98" x 98", 1987, hand pieced and hand quilted. By 1987, Hoffman Fabrics was thrilling quilters with wonderful prints inspired by antique woodblock textiles, and stripes were finally becoming easier to find.

The inspiration for this quilt came from a few of those fabrics, including one that had several widths and varieties of stripes printed as one fabric. The beautiful center block is one of Marsha McCloskey's Feathered-Star variations. Rarely do I limit my palette to just two colors, but in this case, the wide variety of greens, reds, and neutral prints made this quilt extremely fun to design and stitch.

The Eagle and the Rose, 48" x 52", 2004, hand appliquéd and hand quilted. I have always been intrigued by the design similarities between woven coverlets and quilts, especially among the Pennsylvania Germans. Indigo-and-white coverlets seem closely connected to design conventions we see in blue and white quilts, beginning in the second quarter of the 1800s, such as tree and house borders, sunbursts, eagles, roses, and the oak leaf and reel designs.

This small piece is my interpretation of an antique Pennsylvania German quilt dating from about 1850 that was probably inspired by designs seen in a woven coverlet. It is unusual because the appliqués are in white on a blue ground rather than the more common blue on a white ground.

1876 Centennial Medallion, 89" x 89", 2005, hand pieced, hand appliquéd, and hand quilted. During the 1876 celebration of our country's centennial, fabric companies produced a wide variety of patriotic cotton prints that found their way into quilts made during that time. Rusty orange and brown madder-dyed colors, and synthetically dyed Perkin's purple prints were the rage. This quilt showcases many of these fabrics, which have been reproduced during the past several years. The design combines a variation of my favorite Georgetown Circle pattern in the center, with Double Hearts appliqué borders. Of special interest is the print portraying a portrait of George Washington, which is featured in the center and outer corner blocks.

Meeting of the Sunbonnets, 90" x 90", 1986, hand pieced, hand appliquéd, and hand quilted. Both of my daughters loved the Sunbonnet quilts I stitched for them. This one was made for Molly, and it contains all of my favorite Sunbonnet Sue and Overall Bill patterns. It was so fun to stitch so many different versions of the favored pair, rather than repeating just one design over and over in a block-style quilt. Combining them in a medallion format with houses and checkerboard streets seemed the perfect way to show all those busy little people at work and play.

Tree of Paradise Medallion, 102" x 102", 1985, hand pieced, hand appliquéd, and hand quilted. When I began piecing the Delectable Mountain blocks, I had no idea they would end up as the outer border in this medallion. It wasn't until several blocks were finished that I began to visualize them set on point with the exciting purple and rust paisley stripe. A large Tree of Paradise block continued the scrappy feel of the Delectable Mountains and created the perfect center focus.

At the time I was making this quilt, we were just beginning to be able to find border stripes, and the purple paisley striped fabric was special and unusual. Because I wanted to use this fabric as setting strips, I drafted the center tree after the blocks were set together. This quilt was extremely challenging to draft because I was limited by the width of the stripes and had to draft from the edges toward the center. The appliqué border of six-pointed stars and diamonds can be found on English medallion quilts.

Presidents' Medallion,

84" x 84", 2004, hand pieced, hand appliquéd, and hand quilted. Inspired by a unique presidential portrait fabric, this quilt includes many of the reproduction and newly designed patriotic prints that have been available to quiltmakers since the tragedy of September 11, 2001.

For many years, I wanted to make a quilt portraying all of our presidents, but I couldn't decide how to do the portraits. When I found the fabric containing all the presidents, the answer was there, and I began this quilt, which had been in the background of my mind for so long.

The tassel and swag border, a popular motif seen in home furnishings of the Federal period, is frequently used on floral appliqué quilts. But in this case, it seemed to make the perfect finishing statement for this stately, formal, pieced design.

The eagle in the center was cut from a special piece of fabric purchased by my mother in 1976 at the time of our nation's bicentennial celebrations.

For Baby ca. 1850, 48" x 48", 2001, hand pieced, hand appliquéd, and hand quilted. Here's a good example of repeating the colors in the border that were used in the center of the quilt.

A central medallion quilt top, appliquéd with simple folk-art shapes, dated circa 1850, inspired this small piece. Quilting designs and fabrics were chosen that could have been used by quiltmakers in 1850. This piece represents quilts that were stitched as the older central medallion and chintz quilts gave way to the more modern red and green folk-art appliqué block-style quilts. A narrow, straight-of-grain binding was selected to duplicate a binding style popular during this time period.

Early Chintz Medallion, 88" x 91", 1983, machine pieced and hand quilted. Early textile history caught my imagination from the first. I began to search for unusual, hard-to-find cotton fabrics that resembled the early Indian imports to Europe. I stitched this quilt from fabrics found mostly in the 1970s, trying to create what I imagined an early medallion would have looked like.

I used many fabric treasures I had been saving for something special. Having only small pieces of some of the stripes encouraged my creativity, in the same way many early quiltmakers had to make do with what they had.

ABOVE: **Orange Peel Medallion**, 83" x 91", 1982–2005, hand pieced, hand appliquéd, and hand quilted. This quilt began with the beautiful toile from Holland, and it contains numerous English and American indigo scraps from the author's collection. The central laurel wreath can be seen in antique quilts of the British Isles and America.

Mama's Garden, 41" x 52", 2003, hand pieced, hand appliquéd, and hand quilted. Pieced and appliquéd with reproduction fabrics from the 1930s, this child-sized medallion quilt celebrates delightful sunflowers and birds found in summer gardens.

Medallion Quilt Patterns

Presented here are patterns for four medallion quilts. They are organized in order of the skill level needed, proceeding from intermediate to advanced. Be sure to read all the instructions and options before cutting fabrics for your selected design.

Remember that you can substitute simpler blocks if you have not yet mastered advanced piecing and appliqué skills. The beauty of medallion quilts is that you can manipulate, change, and create your own arrangements for the center and the borders while still maintaining the integrity of the overall design.

Early American Medallion

QUILT SIZE: 59½" x 59½"

SKILL LEVEL: early intermediate

SKILLS NEEDED: basic piecing, fitting borders

EARLY AMERICAN MEDALLION, 1996, was machine pieced and hand appliquéd. Inspired by a quilt top pieced in Virginia about 1790, this design combines elements from English frame quilts of the period with an emerging American enthusiasm for star patterns. EARLY AMERICAN MEDALLION was made with reproduction fabrics (printed in 1996) from the Copp textile collection in the Smithsonian Institution. In the late 1700s, this quilt style would have been pieced by a woman of means, with leisure time and access to the expensive imported fabrics that were available on the east coast of America shortly after the War of Independence.

The large corner squares, triangles, and print borders are excellent places to use some of the wonderful large-scale reproduction chintz and striped fabrics available today. This quilt can easily be enlarged by adding an 8" to 10" print border.

Materials

Yardage is based on fabric at least 40" wide.
Cut strips selvage to selvage unless otherwise marked.

fabric	yards	pieces
Burgundy stripe	1⅛	1 A, 12 Q
border 1 (cut parallel to selvages)		4 strips 2" x 16"
border 5 (cut parallel to selvages)		4 strips 3¼" x 37½"
Dk. flowered print	¾	8 C, 16 L, 96 R
Lt. green stripe	½	4 B, 36 M, 8 U
Lt. flowered print	⅝	4 E, 32 M, 4 N
Med. lt. flowered print	1	4 D, 48 R, 48 S
Brown stripe	1¾	16 X
border 3		4 strips 2¼" x 26½"
binding		7 strips 2½" x 40"
Lt. gold print	½	4 F, 16 G, 8 I, 8 V, 8 W
Lt. cream stripe	¼	20 G
Dk. pink print	⅝	36 G, 4 H, 4 H reverse, 4 K, 4 O
Tan print	1	8 C, 16 L, 32 S, 32 T, 8 U
Med. green print	⅝	4 J, 4 P, 8 S, 32 T
Backing	4	2 panels 34" x 67"
Batting	—	67" x 67"

Rotary & Template Cutting

patch	measurements
A	6" x 6"
B	6¾" x 6¾", cut twice diagonally
C	3⅝" x 3⅝", cut once diagonally
D	4⅜" x 4⅜"
E	9" x 9", cut twice diagonally
F	2" x 2"
G–J	Use templates on page 64
K	2¼" x 2¼"
L–O	Use templates on page 65
P	3¼" x 3¼"
Q–T	Use templates on page 66
U	2½" x 2½"
V	1½" x 4½"
W	1½" x 6½"
X	5⅛" x 5⅛", cut once diagonally

Quilt assembly. Measurements shown are finished sizes and do not include seam allowances.

Quilt Assembly

1. As they are needed, cut the fabric pieces listed in the Materials chart on page 60. (See the Rotary and Template Cutting chart for patch measurements and template location.)

2. Referring to figure 1, piece the Northumberland Star center block.

3. Sew border-1 strips to the two sides of the center block. Sew an F square to each end of the remaining two border-1 strips, then sew these strips to the top and bottom of the center block.

4. For border 2, piece four zigzag border strips and four zigzag corner units, as shown in figure 2. Add the zigzag border strips to all four sides of the quilt, followed by the corner units.

5. Sew the four border-3 strips and four K squares to the quilt as you did for border 1.

6. For border 4, piece four diamond border strips and four diamond corner units (fig. 3). Add the diamond border strips to all four sides of the quilt and then the corner units.

7. Sew the four border-5 strips and four P squares to the quilt as before.

8. For border 6, make twelve Variable Star blocks, eight Shoo Fly blocks, and four Four-Patch corner blocks (fig. 4).

9. Join three Variable Star and two Shoo Fly blocks for each border strip (fig. 5). Sew the side borders to the quilt.

Add a Four-Patch corner block to the ends of the remaining two border strips. Sew these strips to the top and bottom of the quilt.

Finishing

1. Sew the backing panels together along their length. Layer the backing, batting, and quilt top, then baste the layers.

2. Outline quilt the patches ½" from the seams. In addition, use the patterns given on pages 67–69, or your favorite quilting patterns, to finish quilting the layers.

3. Use the binding strips and your favorite binding technique to cover the raw edges of the quilt.

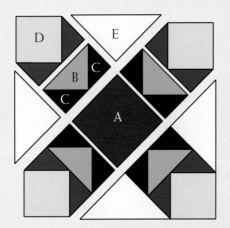

Fig. 1. Northumberland Star center block, finishes 15½" square

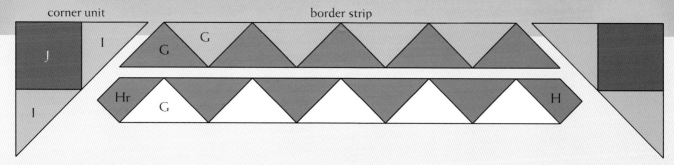

Fig. 2. Zigzag for border 2

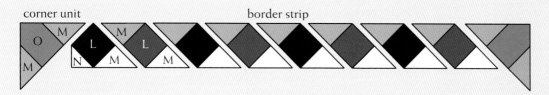

Fig. 3. Diamond strip for border 4

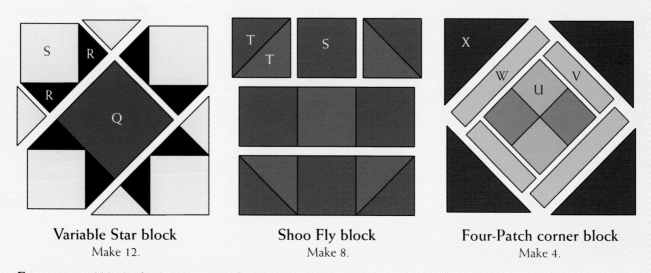

Variable Star block
Make 12.

Shoo Fly block
Make 8.

Four-Patch corner block
Make 4.

Fig. 4. Pieced blocks (finish 8½" square) for border 6

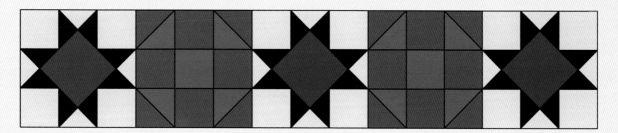

Fig. 5. Border-6 strip

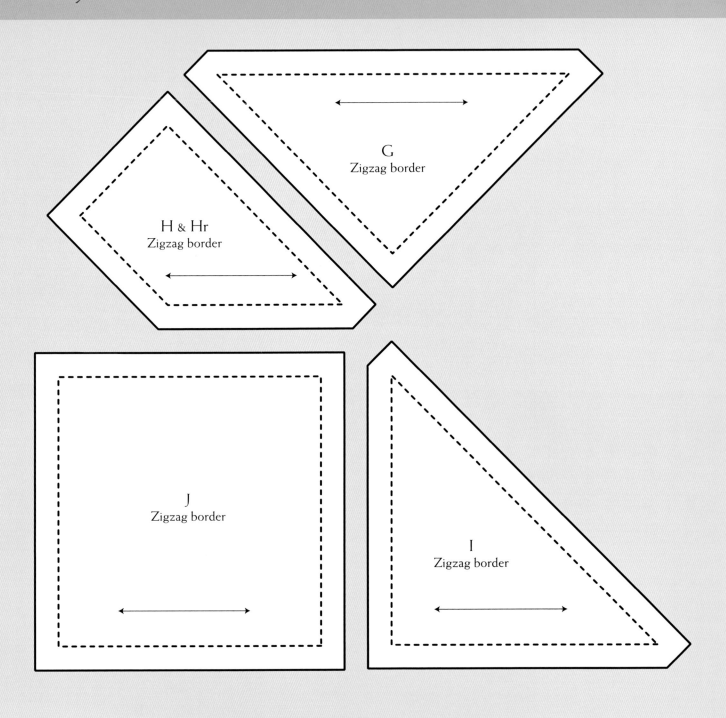

G
Zigzag border

H & Hr
Zigzag border

J
Zigzag border

I
Zigzag border

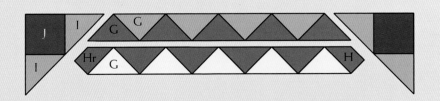

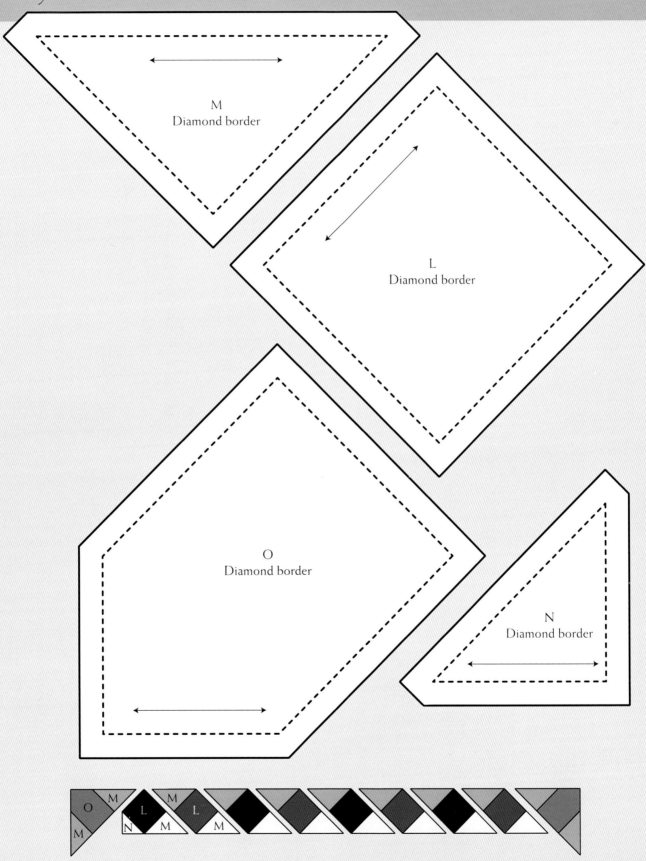

M
Diamond border

L
Diamond border

O
Diamond border

N
Diamond border

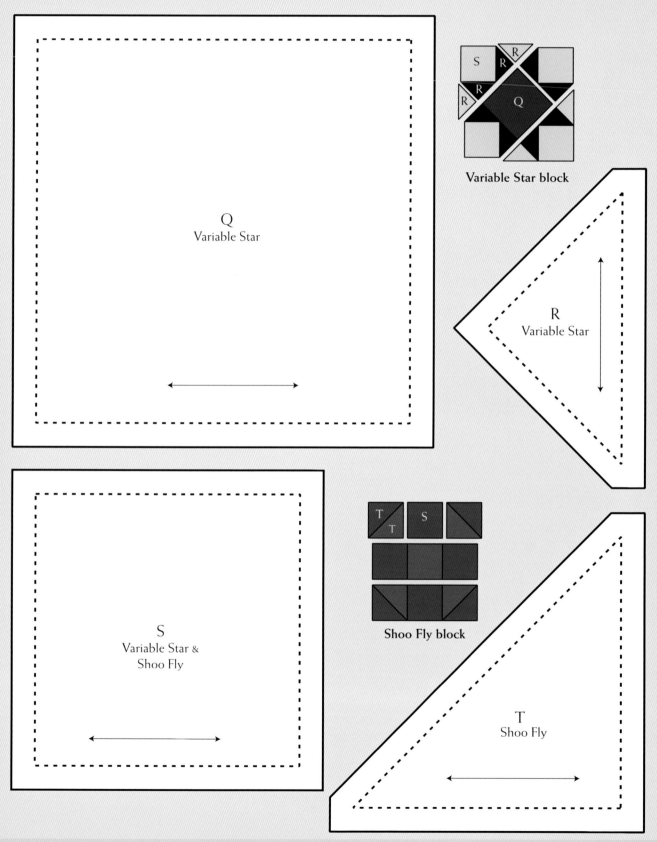

Variable Star block

Q
Variable Star

R
Variable Star

S
Variable Star &
Shoo Fly

Shoo Fly block

T
Shoo Fly

Q, S & U
patches

D & U
patches

X
patch

A
patch

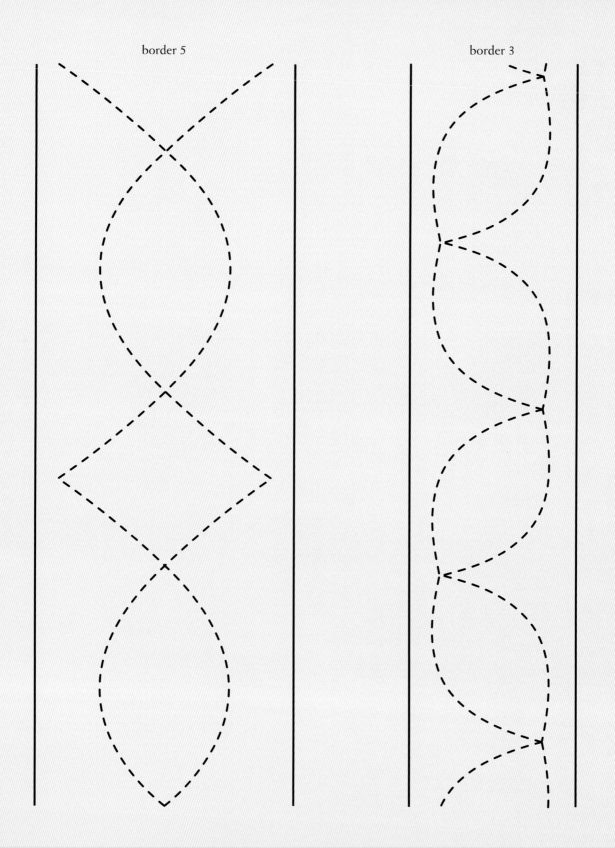

border 5

border 3

English Hearts Medallion

QUILT SIZE: 99" x 99"
SKILL LEVEL: intermediate
SKILLS NEEDED: basic piecing, appliqué, fitting borders, mitering corners

ENGLISH HEARTS MEDALLION, 1985–2005, was hand and machine pieced, hand appliquéd, and hand quilted.

Among my favorite designs are the heart patterns that appear frequently in nineteenth-century quilts made in the British Isles. Hearts are used as quilting patterns and as appliqué motifs, both in center medallions and in smaller corner motifs. American quilters freely adapted these designs, and we have come to associate them with the arts and crafts of the Pennsylvania Germans.

My quilt originated from a desire to use a packet of fabric squares given to me by a dear friend, who had visited a quilt shop in England. In the early 1980s, when this top was made, there were few antique-looking fabrics on the market. One of the first wood-block-reproduction stripes printed by Hoffman provided the perfect print borders for this quilt. The English fabrics my friend brought me had a different look about them, compared to the American fabrics available at that time; the scale of the prints was larger and the colors were more muted and aged.

English Hearts Medallion

Materials Yardage is based on fabric at least 40″ wide. Cut strips selvage to selvage unless otherwise marked.		
fabric	**yards**	**pieces**
White	3⅜″	
center block background		1 square 37″ x 37″
orange peel border		2 strips 9½″ x 59½″
		2 strips 9½″ x 75½″
Med. green & pink print	1	1 A, 4 E
Rose	¼	4 D
Stripe	4¾	
border 1		4 strips 3″ x 42½″
border 3		4 strips 3½″ x 58½″
border 5		4 strips 4½″ x 82½″
border 7		4 strips 5″ x 101½″
Scraps	5½ total	36 B, 264 C, 128 F, 272 G
Backing	9½	3 panels 37″ x 107″
Batting	—	107″ x 107″
Binding	1	11 strips 2½″ x 40″

Rotary & Template Cutting	
patch	**measurements**
A–B	use templates on page 76
C	6¼″ x 6¼″, cut twice diagonally
D	5½″ x 5½″
E–F	use templates on page 77
G	2¼″ x 2¼″

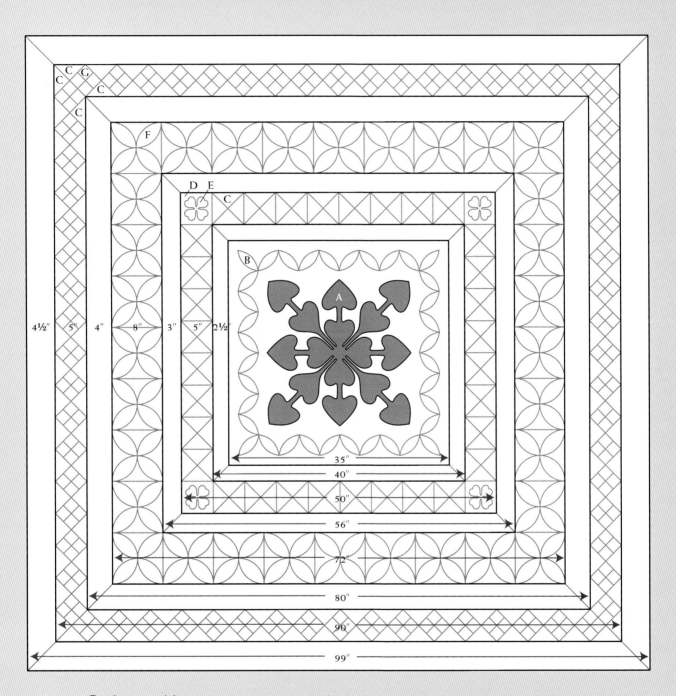

Quilt assembly. Measurements shown are finished sizes and do not include seam allowances.

Quilt Assembly

1. As they are needed, cut the fabric pieces listed in the Materials chart on page 72. (See the Rotary and Template Cutting chart for the patch measurements and template locations.)

2. Prepare the appliqué background and fabric pieces. Referring to the quilt photo and quilt assembly diagram (page 73) for placement, appliqué the center block. Trim the block to 35½" square.

3. Sew the four border-1 strips to the center square and miter the corners. Trim any extra border length.

4. For border 2, piece four Broken Dishes border strips (fig. 1). Appliqué the four Shamrock corner squares (pieces D and E). Sew a border strip to the two sides of the quilt. Sew a corner square to each end of

the remaining two border strips. Sew these strips to the top and bottom.

5. Sew the four border-3 strips to the quilt and miter the corners. Trim any extra border length.

6. To mark orange-peel guidelines for border 4, fold each white strip in half lengthwise and press, then fold crosswise and press. For each short strip, mark seven 8" sections (fig. 2). For each long strip, mark nine 8" sections.

7. Appliqué the orange peel sections to the four border strips. Trim all four strips to 8½" wide. Trim the shorter strips to 56½" in length and the longer strips to 72½".

8. Sew the short appliquéd strips to the sides of the quilt and the long strips to the top and bottom. Add the four border-5 strips to the quilt as before.

9. For border 6, make 68 scrappy four-patch units. Add C patches to the four-patch units to make 56 side units and four end units. Also make four corner units (fig. 3).

10. Sew 14 side units and one end unit together to make each of the four border strips (fig. 4). Pay special attention to the placement of the end units.

11. Sew the Four-Patch border strips to the quilt and add the four corner units. Add the four border-7 strips to the quilt as before to complete the quilt top.

Finishing

1. Sew the backing panels (minus selvages) together along their length. Layer the backing, batting, and quilt top, then baste the layers.

2. Use the patterns given on pages 79–81, or your favorite quilting patterns, to quilt the layers.

3. Use the binding strips to cover the raw edges of the quilt.

Appliquéing the Hearts

Appliqué the outermost hearts first, leaving the interior hearts and stems uncut until you are ready to stitch those areas.

corner   border strip

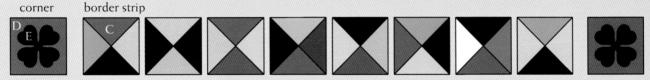

Fig. 1. Broken Dishes blocks (finish 5" square) for border 2

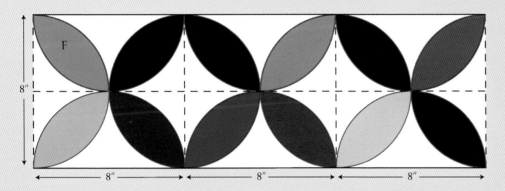

Fig. 2. Guidelines for placing orange peel sections (border 4)

side unit   end unit   corner unit

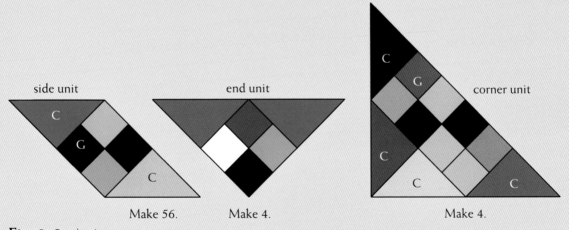

Make 56.   Make 4.   Make 4.

Fig. 3. Border-6 units

end unit

Fig. 4. Four-Patch border strip

⅛ of A
inner heart

Enlarge template A 200%

outer heart

B
full size

Preparing Appliqué Patches

Here is an easy way to turn under the edges of appliqué shapes, such as circles, leaves, and orange peel sections: Cut a firm cardboard template for each shape. Sew a gathering stitch in the turn-under allowance of the fabric piece. Insert the cardboard shape. Pull the thread to gather the edges around the template. Press well with a steam iron. Remove the cardboard shape and pull the gathering thread again, as needed, to tuck under the allowance.

Add ³⁄₁₆" turn-under allowance to appliqué pieces.

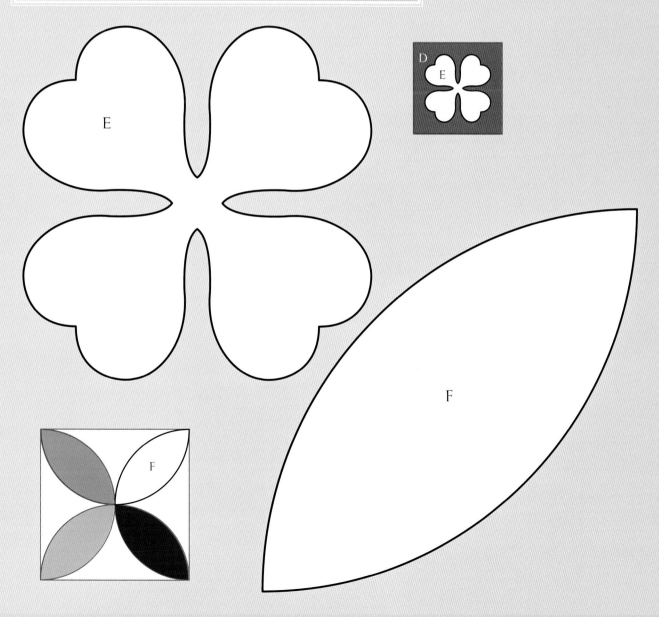

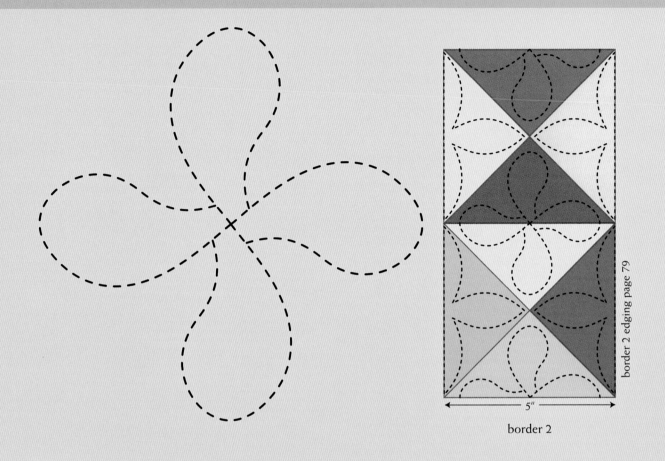

border 2 edging page 79

5"

border 2

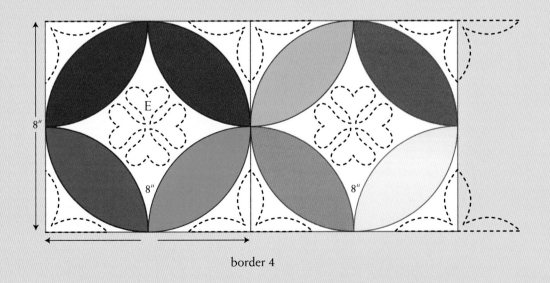

8"

E

8"

8"

border 4

border 2 edging

C
patch

E
patch

outer edge of center block

outer heart

inner heart

Welsh Hearts
quilting designs for piece A

Crazy Anne's Fancy

QUILT SIZE: 77½" x 77½"
SKILL LEVEL: advanced intermediate
**SKILLS NEEDED: appliquéing circles and scallops, piecing
five points that meet, piecing mirror images, fitting borders,
mitering corners**

CRAZY ANNE'S FANCY, 2002, was hand pieced, hand appliquéd, and
hand quilted. The vibrant colors, folky appliqué motifs, scalloped borders, and
liberal use of hearts in this medallion quilt are all indications of Pennsylvania
German inspiration. Fabrics in this quilt are reproductions of prints
produced in American textile factories in the last decades of the
nineteenth century. P & B textiles printed this "From The Mills
Collection" in 2001. Samples of the original prints from this
line are in the archives of the American Textile History
Museum in Lowell, Massachusetts.

Small-scale prints work well for the appliqués,
pieced blocks, and background squares. The
unpieced squares provide areas to highlight your best
hand quilting skills. For the scalloped border background,
search for a medium-scale, subtle print that will enhance but
not overpower the scallops and dots.

Materials

Yardage is based on fabric at least 40" wide.
Cut strips selvage to selvage unless otherwise marked.

fabric	yards	pieces
Pink	2¼	Center square, 48 K, 20 Q
Bright blue print	2¼	1 D, 66 K, 8 Q, 4 I
border 1		4 strips 1½" x 22½"
Dk. Blue	¼	48 K, 8 S
Med. multi-colored print	½	1 E
Gold	⅛	4 J, 4 Jr
Red	1⅜	1 B, 4 G, 4 L, 8 T, 4 V
border 3		4 strips 2¼" x 39"
border-6 scallops		8 strips 2¼" x 40"
Yellow	1¾	1 A, 66 K, 112 N, 224 P, 8 R
border-2 scallops		4 strips 2½" x 25½"
Green	¾	4 F, 8 U
Scraps (include bright blue)	1⅝ total	140 M, 112 Nr, 112 O
Medium-scale dark print	3⅛	1C, 4 H
border 2		4 strips 5½" x 36½"
border 6 (cut parallel to selvages)		6" x 80"
Backing	7½	3 panels 29" x 85½"
Batting	—	85½" x 85½"
Binding	¾	9 strips 2½" x 40'

Rotary & Template Cutting

patch	measurements
A	2¼" x 2¼"
B	4½" x 4½"
C–L	Use templates on pages 88–92
M	2" x 2"
N–Nr	2¼" x 4½", cut once diagonally
O	3⅞" x 3⅞"
P	2⅜" x 2⅜"
Q	8" x 8"
R–U	Use templates on page 91
V	1½" x 1½"

Quilt assembly. Measurements shown are finished sizes and do not include seam allowances.

Quilt Assembly

1. As they are needed, cut the fabric pieces listed in the Materials chart on page 84. (See the Rotary and Template Cutting chart for patch measurements and template locations.)

2. For the quilt center, prepare the background and appliqué pieces. Referring to the quilt assembly diagram on page 85 for placement, appliqué the center block. Trim the block to 22½" square.

3. For border 1, sew bright blue strips to the two sides of the quilt. Add a red square (V patch) to each end of the remaining two border strips and sew them to the top and bottom of the quilt.

4. Prepare and pin a yellow scallop strip to the inner edge of a border-2 strip, matching centers. Appliqué the scallops to the border strip then add the dots (K). Make four

border strips like this. Sew the strips to the quilt and miter the corners. Trim any extra border length. Appliqué a heart (L patch) over each corner seam.

5. Sew the four red border-3 strips to the quilt and miter the corners. Trim any extra border length.

6. For borders 4 and 5, make 28 Crazy Anne blocks and eight appliqué corner blocks (fig. 1).

7. Join three Crazy Anne blocks with two print squares (Q) to make each border-4 strip (fig. 2).

8. Sew border-4 strips to the two sides of the quilt. Sew an appliqué corner block to each end of the remaining two border strips then sew them to the top and bottom of the quilt.

9. For each border-5 strip, join four Crazy Anne blocks

and three print squares (fig. 3). Repeat step 8 to add border 5 to the quilt.

10. For border 6, join two red scallop strips, end to end, for each side of the quilt. Mark the scallop pattern on each border strip (Be sure the seam falls between two scallops.)

11. Appliqué a scallop strip to the inner edge of each border-6 strip, matching their centers. Add a dot (K) to each scallop. Sew the four border strips to the quilt and miter the corners. Trim any excess border length.

Finishing

1. Sew the backing panels together along their length. Layer the backing, batting, and quilt top, then baste the layers.

2. Outline-quilt the patches ¼" from the seams. In addition, use the patterns given on page 93, or your favorite quilting patterns, to finish quilting the layers.

3. Use the binding strips and your favorite binding technique to cover the raw edges of the quilt.

Simple Dot Template

Except for the center circle, all dots are the size of a 25-cent piece, which makes a perfect template to draw circles on fabric.

Mirror-Image Blocks

Note that some Crazy Anne blocks swirl to the left and others to the right. This is because the long triangles (N/Nr patches) become a mirror image when cut two at a time from folded fabric. If you want all blocks the same, cut pieces N & Nr from fabrics all face up or all face down.

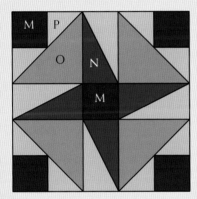

Crazy Anne block

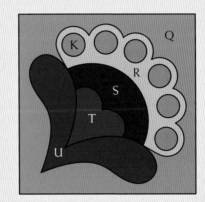

Appliqué corner block

Fig. 1. Crazy Anne block and appliqué corner block

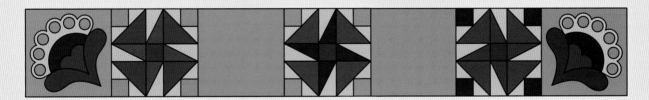

Fig. 2. Border-4 strip

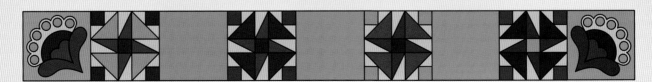

Fig. 3. Border-5 strip

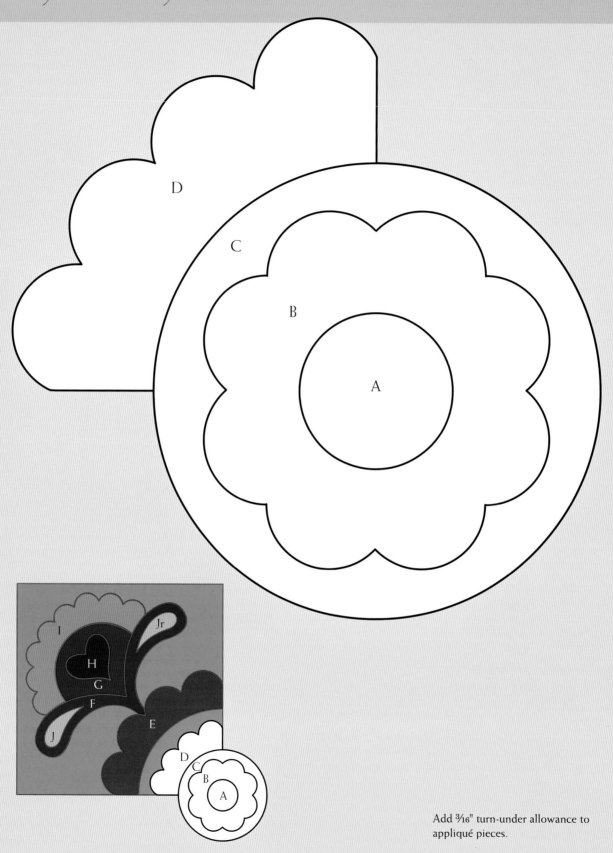

Add ³⁄₁₆" turn-under allowance to appliqué pieces.

I

E

Add ³⁄₁₆" turn-under allowance to appliqué pieces.

Add ³⁄₁₆" turn-under allowance to appliqué pieces.

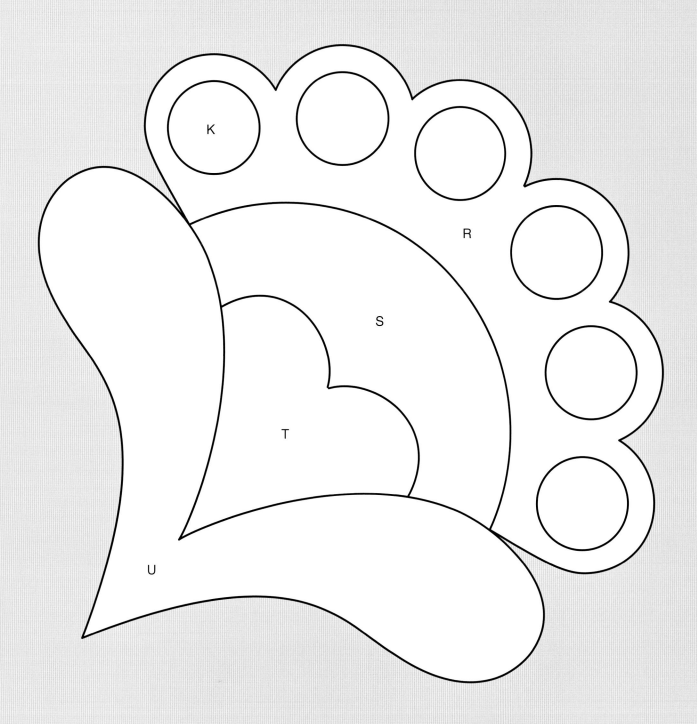

Add ³⁄₁₆" turn-under allowance to appliqué pieces.

L

Add ³⁄₁₆" turn-under allowance to appliqué pieces.

K

Scallop pattern

Use 4 in each
plain square.

plain square

quilt center

quilt center

corner of quilt center

Friskey's Garden

QUILT SIZE: 95" x 95"
SKILL LEVEL: advanced
SKILLS NEEDED: curved piecing, set-in seams, appliquéd circles and curves, working with many templates and small pieces, mirror-image appliqués, fitting borders

FRISKEY'S GARDEN, 2002, was hand and machine pieced, hand appliquéd, and hand quilted. Inspiration to make this quilt flooded through me one August morning as I walked through a Colorado meadow accompanied by my feline companion, Friskey. Deep, rich colors, smells of the moist earth and green growing leaves, and vibrant patches of golden yellow sunflowers filled me with joy and contentment. Sweet bird songs wafting from the surrounding forest and light from the rising sun completed the perfect beauty of the place. My dear cat frolicked by my side in the lush grass. All was right with the world, and I wanted to capture this moment forever.

Quiltmakers have always known that even in deepest winter, a quilt such as this can bring the warmth of an August summer's day into heart and home.

Materials

Yardage is based on fabric at least 42" wide.
Cut strips selvage to selvage unless otherwise marked.

fabric	yards	pieces
Light brown plaid	¾	6 strips 3½" x 42" (see steps 2 & 3)
Light tan print	¾	6 strips 3½" x 42" (see steps 2 & 3)
Scraps	7¾ total	leaves, flowers, pods, cats, and birds
Greens	⅞ total	bias stems
Dark brown & rust paisley	2½	48 A, 4 B, 200 C, 4 D (dogtooth borders 1–3)
Light brown stripe	⅝	52 A (dogtooth border 1)
Light beige stripe	⅞	84 C (dogtooth border 2)
Medium orange stripe	1⅜	116 C, 4 D (dogtooth border 3)
Gold background print	3¼	4 corner triangles (see step 7)
Brown plaid border	2¼	4 strips 10" x 68½" (cut parallel to selvages)
Backing	9	3 panels 35" x 103"
Batting	—	103" x 103"
Binding	⅞	11 strips 2½" x 40"

Template Cutting

templates	page
Center Sunflower appliqué	101–105
Dogtooth borders	106–107
Corner triangle appliqué	108–109
Top border appliqué	110–114
Bottom border appliqué	115–117
Side border appliqué	118–120
Sunflower corner appliqué	121

Quilt assembly. Measurements shown are finished size and do not include seam allowance.

3½"

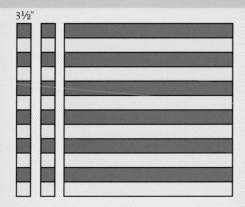

Fig. 1. Center background strip-set

Fig. 2. Completed background

Quilt Assembly

1. As they are needed, cut the fabric pieces listed in the Materials chart. (Appliqué and piecing templates are on pages 101–121).

2. To strip-piece the checkerboard Sunflower background, join the six light brown plaid and six light tan print strips, alternating colors, to make a strip-set. Cut the strip-set into twelve segments, each 3½" wide (fig. 1).

3. Join the segments to create the checkerboard background. The square should measure 36½" with seam allowances (fig. 2).

4. Referring to figure 3, piece the center Sunflower petals. Piece the center circle to the petals. (If you prefer, you can appliqué the circle to the petals after they have been pinned to the background.)

5. Position and pin the Sunflower in the center of the background checkerboard. Appliqué the petals to the background. Pin and appliqué the corner leaf-pod-stem motifs in place.

6. Referring to figure 4, piece four dogtooth border-1 strips and four corner units. Join the strips to the quilt center then add the corner units with set-in seams.

7. Cut the gold corner triangles as shown in figure 5. It is important to cut the long edges on the straight of grain to avoid stretching them out of shape. Run a line of machine basting stitches around the bias edges to avoid stretching during the appliqué process.

8. Assemble four of flower 1 and eight of flower 2. Note that some leaves are reversed. Position and appliqué the bias stems, leaves, and flowers on

Fig. 3. Center Sunflower assembly

corner unit   strip

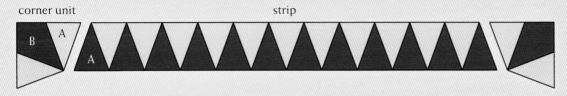

Fig. 4. Dogtooth border 1.

selvage

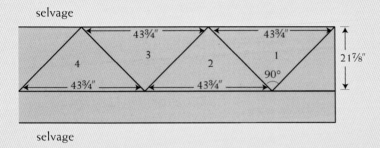

selvage

Fig. 5. Cutting gold corner triangles

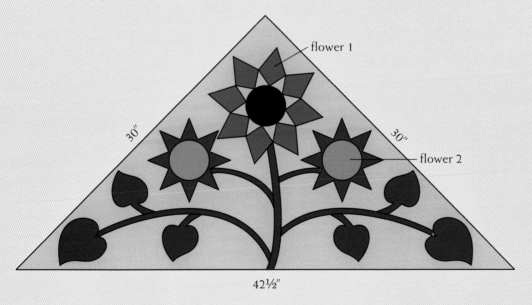

Fig. 6. Corner triangle appliqué

corner unit   strip

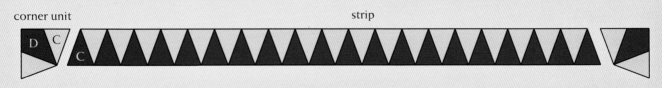

Fig. 7. Dogtooth border 2

the corner triangles, keeping in mind that the finished triangles will be 30" x 42½" (fig. 6). Add the triangles to the quilt then trim them, leaving a ¼" seam allowance.

9. Referring to figure 7 (page 99), piece four dogtooth border-2 strips and four corner units. Join them to the quilt center as before.

10. Referring to the quilt photo and quilt assembly diagram (page 97), appliqué the top, bottom, and side borders, noting that some leaves and pods are reversed.

11. Stitch four corner Sunflower blocks (fig. 8). Options: The center circle can be pieced or appliquéd. The Sunflower can be pieced into the background or appliquéd onto a 10" square.

12. Sew the top and bottom border strips to the quilt. Join the corner Sunflower blocks to the side strips and sew these to the quilt.

13. Referring to the quilt assembly diagram, add the last dogtooth border as before. Each border strip has 30 paisley C pieces and 29 orange C pieces.

Finishing

1. Sew the backing panels together along their length. Layer the backing, batting, and quilt top, then baste the layers.

2. Outline quilt the patches ¼" from the seams. In addition, use the patterns given on pages 122–124, or your favorite quilting patterns, to finish quilting the layers.

3. Use the binding strips and your favorite binding technique to cover the raw edges of the quilt.

Fig. 8. Corner Sunflower assembly

center block

To piece center to petals, add ¼" seam allowance.

To appliqué center, add ³⁄₁₆" turn-under allowance.

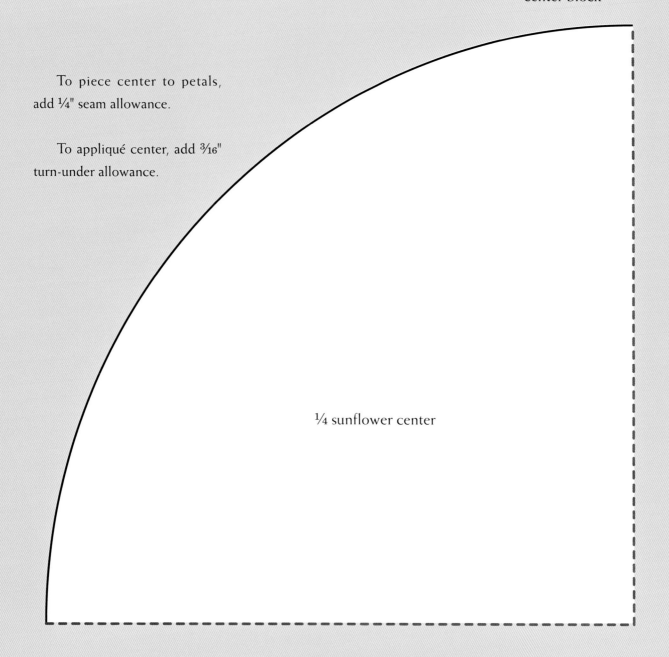

¼ sunflower center

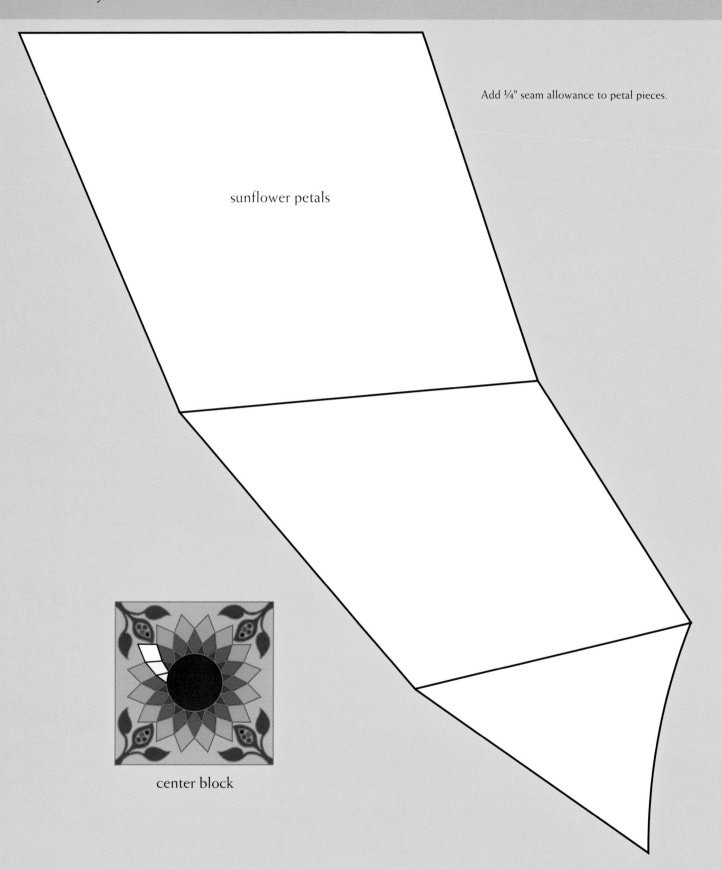

sunflower petals

Add ¼" seam allowance to petal pieces.

center block

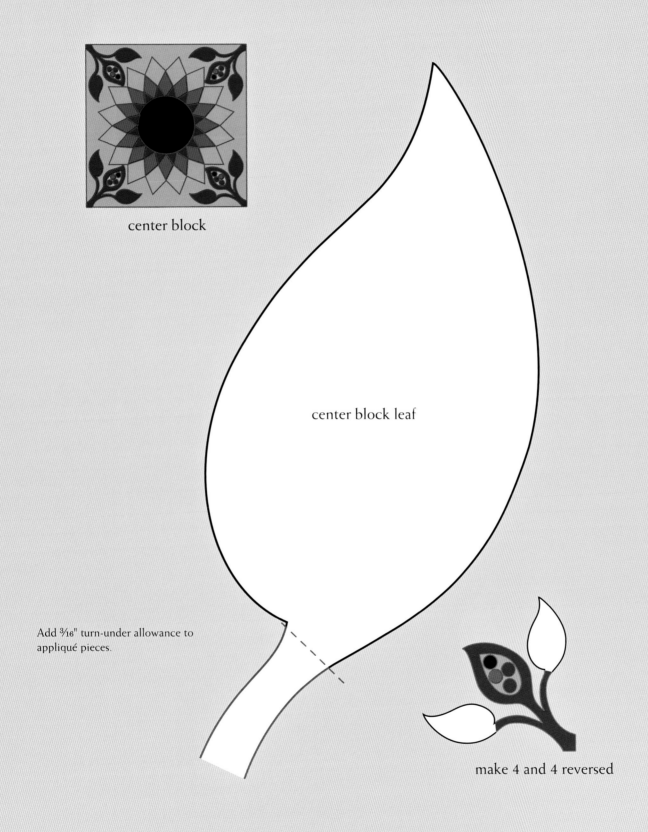

center block

center block leaf

Add ³⁄₁₆" turn-under allowance to appliqué pieces.

make 4 and 4 reversed

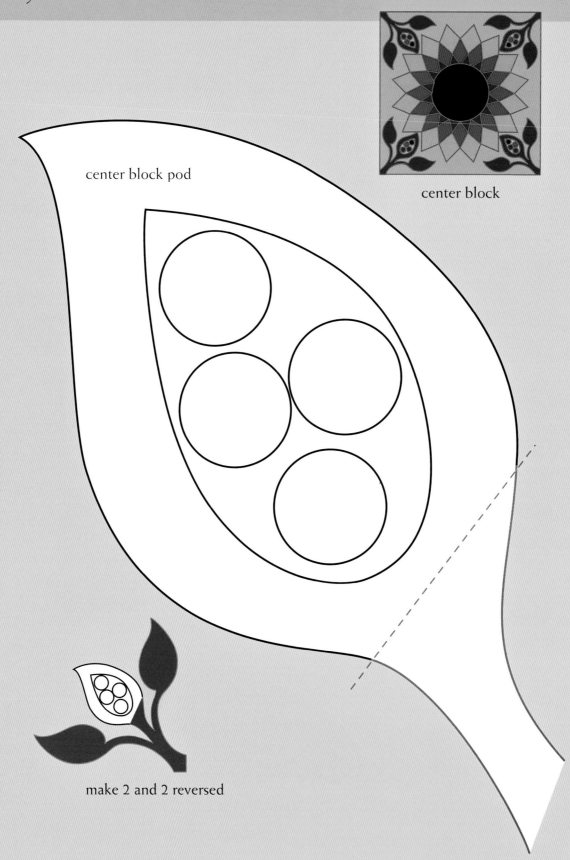

center block

center block pod

make 2 and 2 reversed

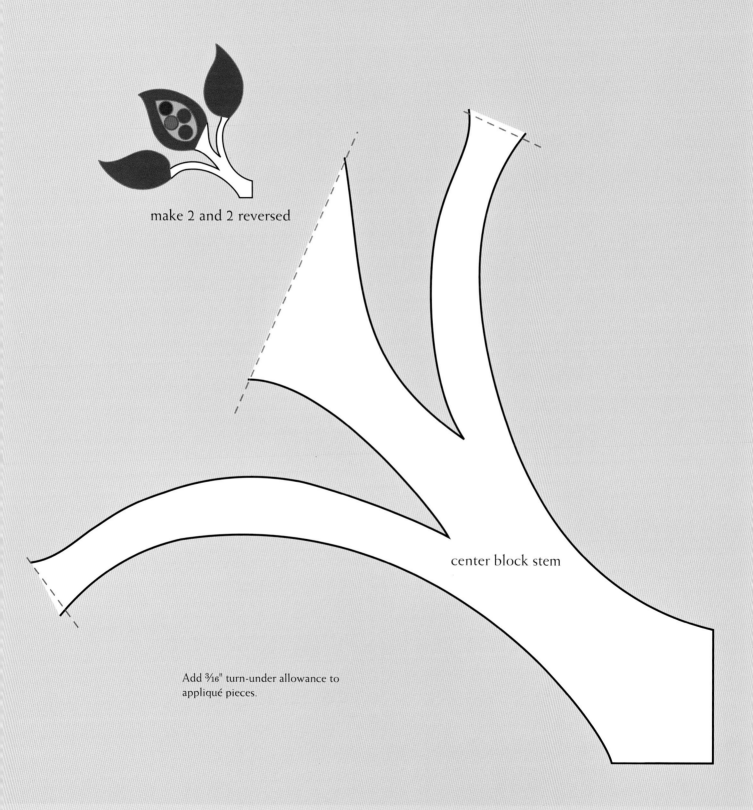

make 2 and 2 reversed

center block stem

Add ³⁄₁₆" turn-under allowance to
appliqué pieces.

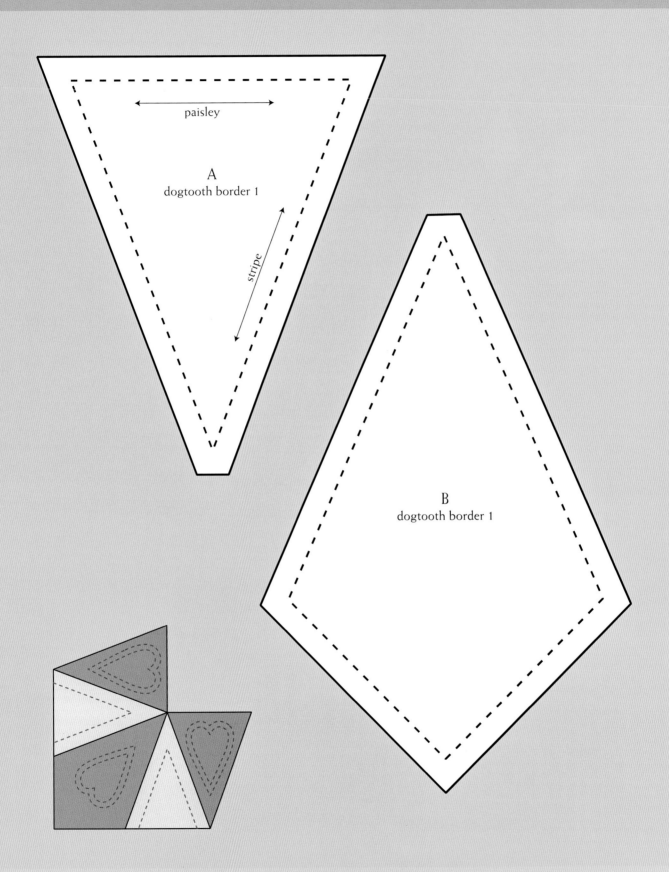

paisley

A
dogtooth border 1

stripe

B
dogtooth border 1

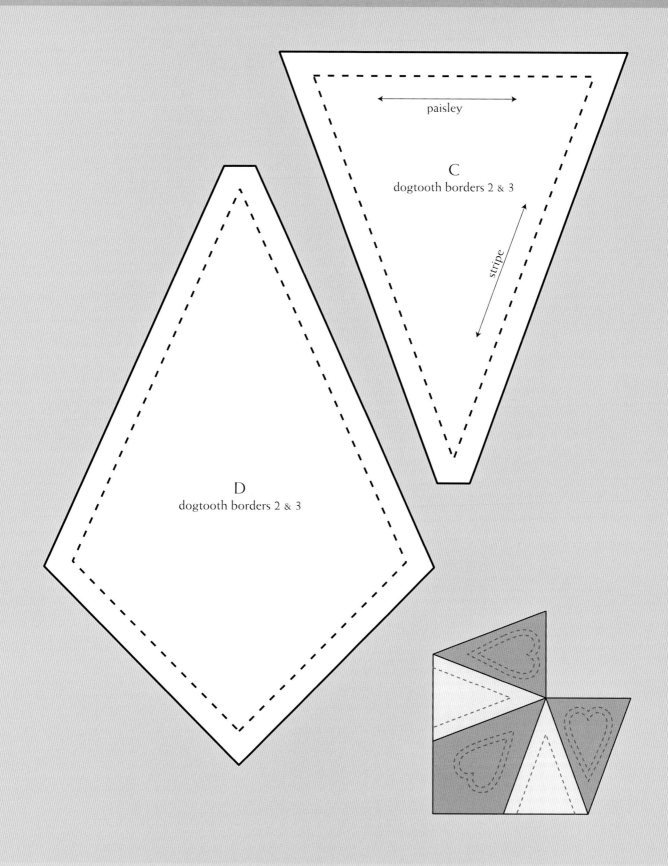

paisley

C
dogtooth borders 2 & 3

stripe

D
dogtooth borders 2 & 3

corner triangle
leaf 1

corner triangle
flower-1 petal

Add ¼" seam allowance to petal pieces.

Add ³⁄₁₆" turn-under allowance to appliqué pieces.

corner triangle
flower-1 center

corner triangle

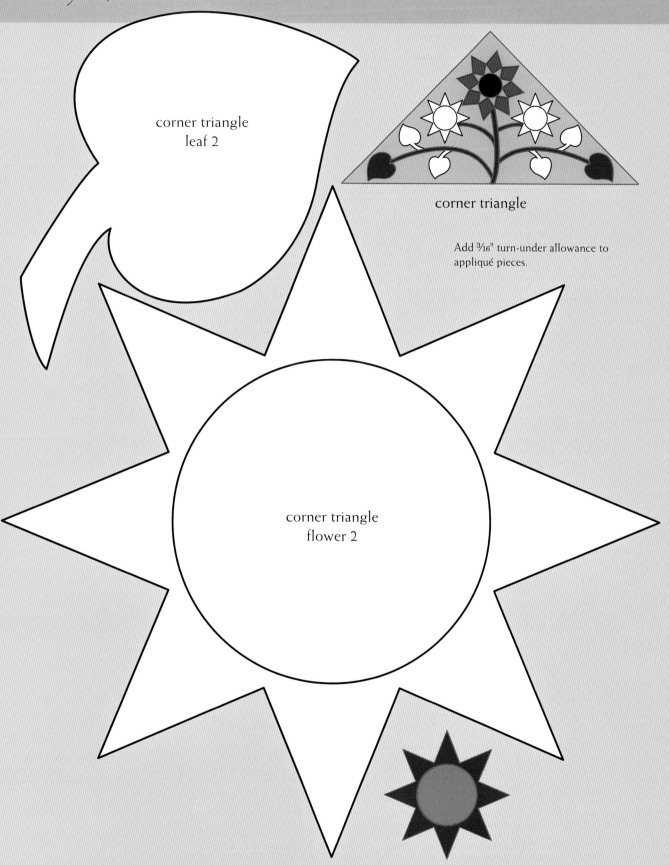

corner triangle
leaf 2

corner triangle

Add ³⁄₁₆" turn-under allowance to
appliqué pieces.

corner triangle
flower 2

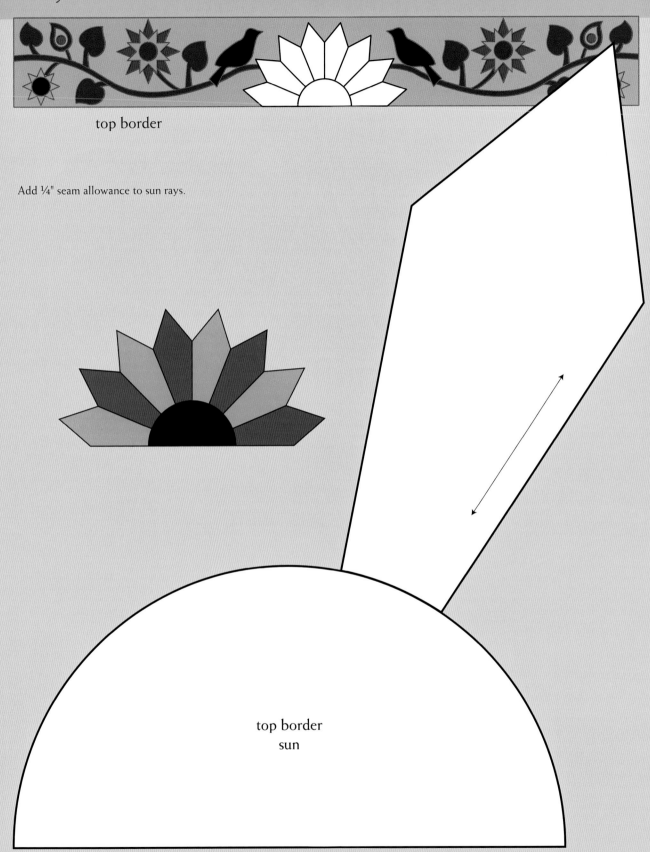

top border

Add ¼" seam allowance to sun rays.

top border
sun

Friskey's Garden patterns

top border

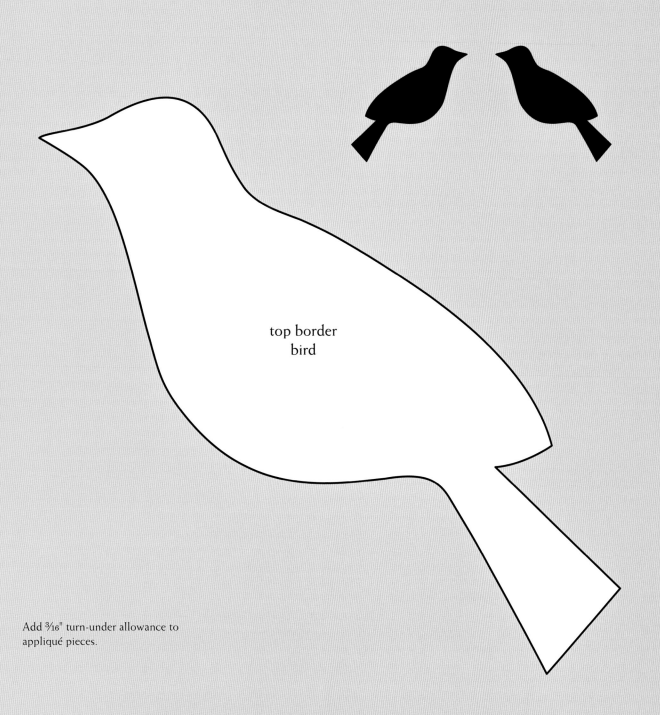

top border
bird

Add ³⁄₁₆" turn-under allowance to
appliqué pieces.

top & bottom borders
flower 3

Friskey's Garden patterns

top border

top border
flower 7

borders
leaf 3

Add ³⁄₁₆" turn-under allowance to
appliqué pieces.

Friskey's Garden patterns

top border

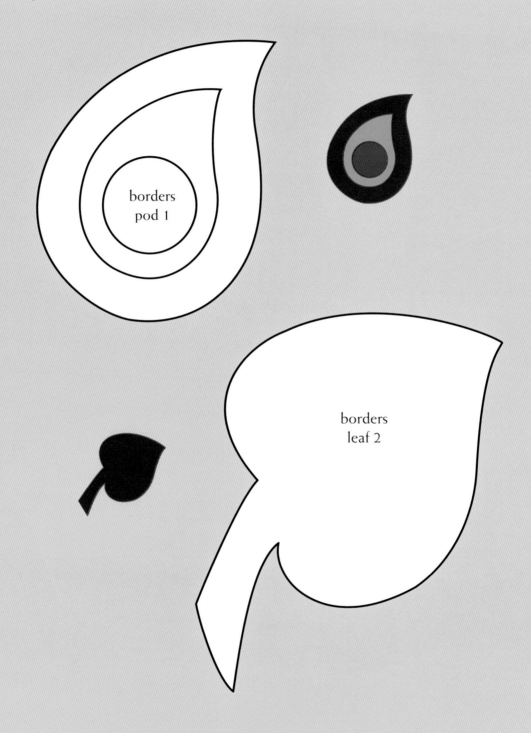

borders
pod 1

borders
leaf 2

Friskey's Garden patterns

bottom border

bottom border
flower 4

Add ³⁄₁₆" turn-under allowance to
appliqué pieces.

bottom border

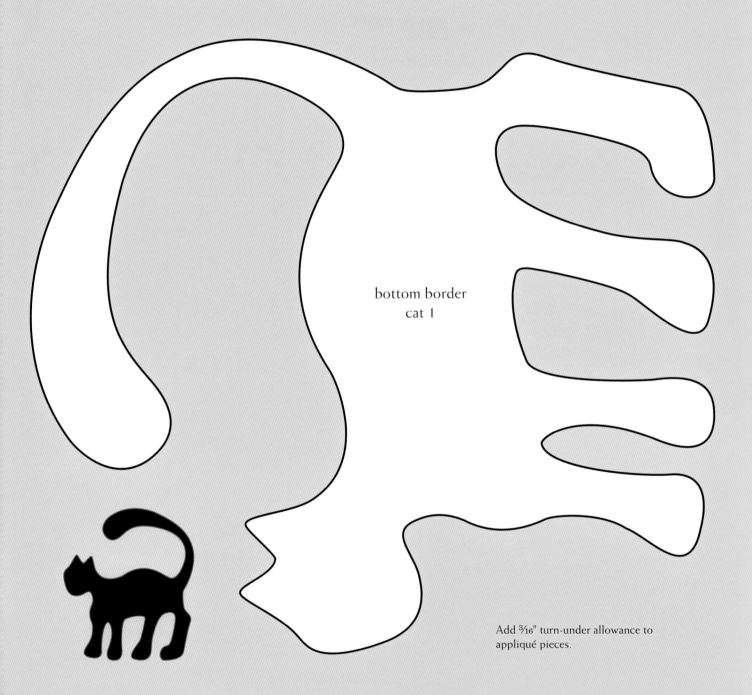

bottom border
cat 1

Add ³⁄₁₆" turn-under allowance to
appliqué pieces.

bottom border

bottom border
cat 2

right side border
(Mirror for left
side border.)

side border
flower 5

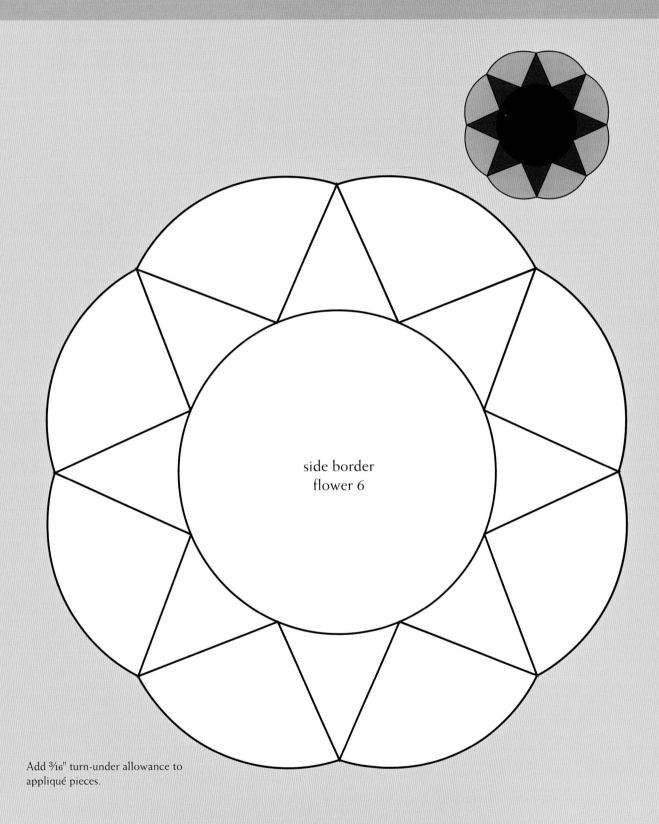

side border
flower 6

Add ³⁄₁₆" turn-under allowance to
appliqué pieces.

Friskey's Garden patterns

right side border

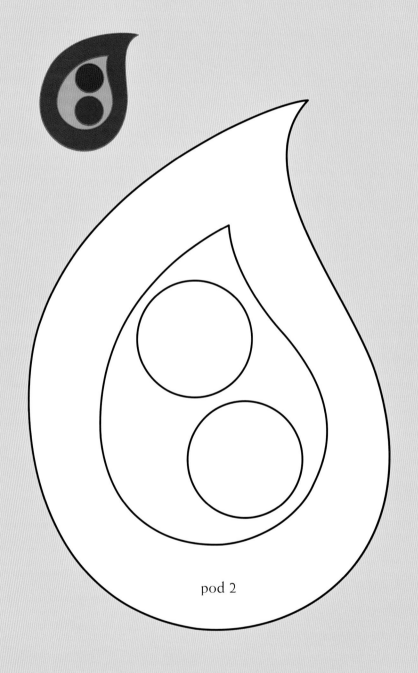

pod 2

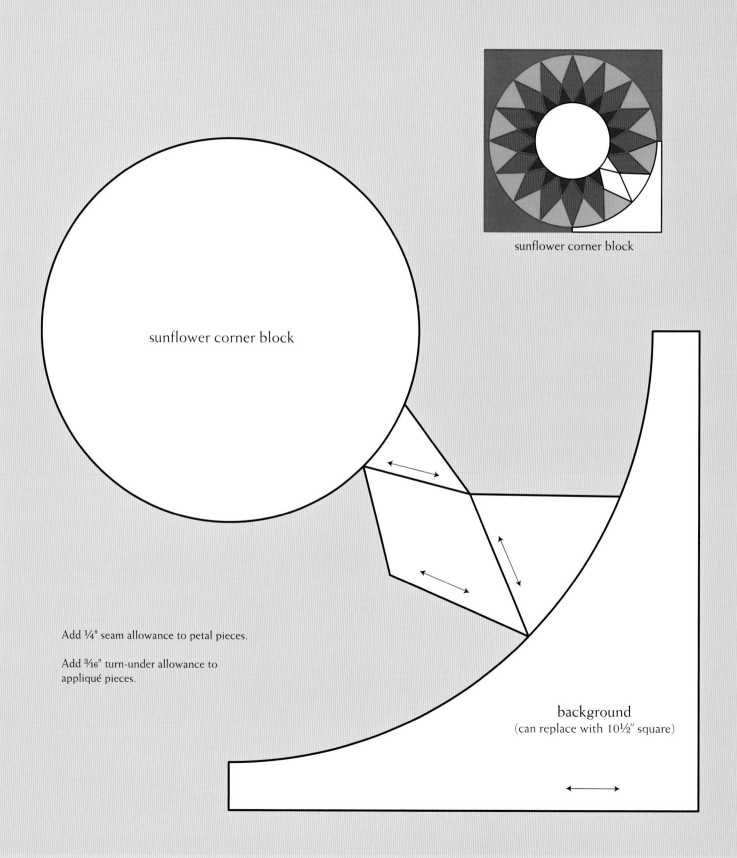

sunflower corner block

sunflower corner block

Add ¼" seam allowance to petal pieces.

Add ³⁄₁₆" turn-under allowance to appliqué pieces.

background
(can replace with 10½" square)

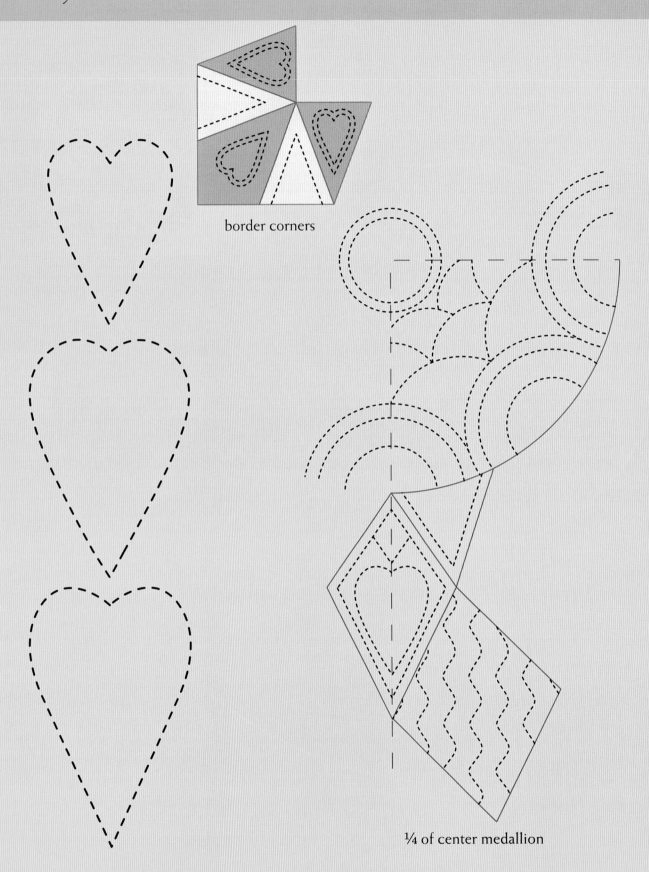

border corners

¼ of center medallion

leaf quilting

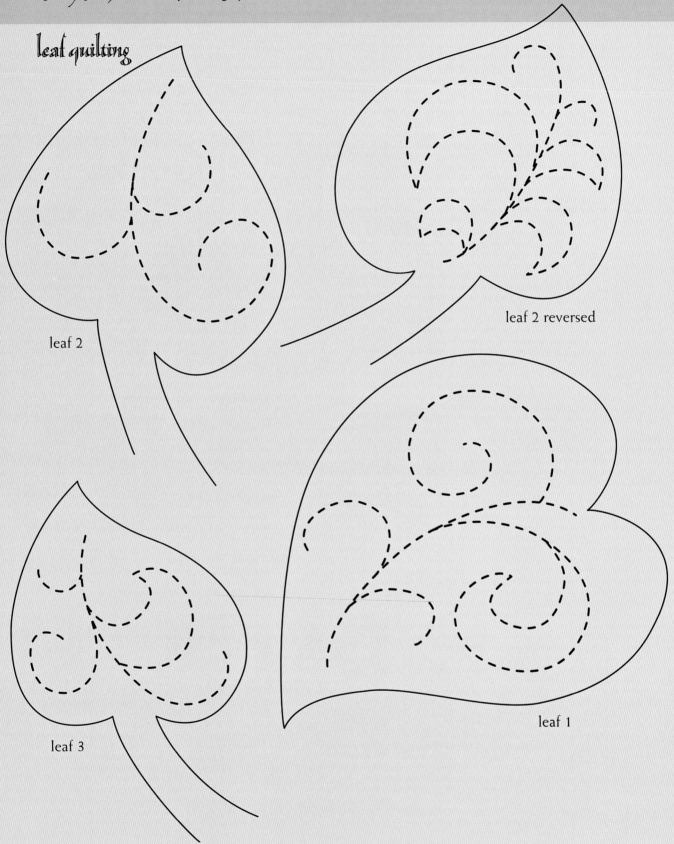

leaf 2

leaf 2 reversed

leaf 3

leaf 1

Bibliography

Allan, Rosemary. *Quilts and Coverlets from Beamish Museum*. Stanley, Co. Durham: Beamish North of England Open Air Museum, 1987.

Beer, Alice Baldwin. *Trade Goods*. Washington, D. C.: Smithsonian Institution Press, 1970.

Beyer, Jinny. *The Art and Technique of Creating Medallion Quilts*. McLean, Virginia: EPM Publications, Inc., 1982.

—. *Patchwork Patterns*. Virginia: EPM Publications, 1979.

—. *Quiltmaking by Hand*. Elmhurst, IL: Breckling Press, 2004.

Colby, Avril. *Patchwork*. London: B. T. Batsford LTD, 1958.

Fox, Sandi. *Quilts In Utah: A Reflection of the Western Experience*. Utah: Salt Lake Art Center, 1981. (exhibition catalog)

Havig, Bettina. *Classic English Medallion Style Quilts*. Paducah, KY: American Quilter's Society, 2003.

Horton, Marjorie. *Welsh Quilting Pattern & Design Handbook*. Self published, 1999.

Johnson, Bruce. *A Child's Comfort: Baby and Doll Quilts in American Folk Art*. New York: Harcourt Brace Jovanovich, 1977.

Kiracofe, Roderick. *The American Quilt: A History of Cloth and Comfort 1750-1950*. New York: Clarkson N. Potter, Inc., 1993.

Marston, Gwen, & Cunningham, Joe. *Quilting with Style: Principles for Great Pattern Design*. Paducah, KY: American Quilter's Society, 1993.

Orlofsky, Patsy and Myron. *Quilts in America*. New York: Abbeville Press, 1974.

Osler, Dorothy. *Quilting Design Sourcebook*. Washington, That Patchwork Place, Inc., 1996.

Martin, Judy, and McCloskey, Marsha. *Pieced Borders: The Complete Resource*. Iowa: Crosley-Griffith Publishing Company, Inc., 1994.

Editors. *McCall's Needlework & Crafts Heirloom Quilts*. New York: The McCall Pattern Company, 1974, p. 7.

Quilt Treasures of Great Britain: The Heritage Search of the Quilters' Guild. London: Deirdre McDonald Books, 1995.

Siegele, Starr. *Toiles for All Seasons: French & English Printed Textiles*. Charlestown, MA: Bunker Hill Publishing, Inc., 2004.

Wagner, Debra. *Striplate Piecing: Piecing Circle Designs with Speed and Accuracy*. Paducah, KY: American Quilter's Society, 1994.

A helpful source for locating out-of-print books is Advanced Book Exchange. www. abebooks.com.

Meet the Author

Passionate about making quilts and a serious scholar of quilt history since the 1960s, Cindy Vermillion Hamilton (formerly Davis) is a self-taught folk artist who brings new life to traditional quilt design with her unique arrangements of color and pattern. Hand-pieced and hand-quilted medallion, sunflower, and sunburst designs are her specialties. This mother of three teaches hand techniques, lectures about her quilts, and continues to contribute patterns and articles to magazines.

Cindy's quilts have won national contests, and they have been shown and patterned in major publications since the early 1970s. Among her proudest achievements are two first-place awards in the traditional pieced professional category, and one second place in the appliqué professional category at the American Quilter's Society show in Paducah, Kentucky.

She has designed quilts for a fabric company, and her work has graced the covers of numerous publications, including two for *Quilter's Newsletter Magazine*. Two museums have her work in their collections: the Allentown Art Museum in Pennsylvania and the Museum of the American Quilter's Society in Paducah.

Her formal education took place at the University of Southern California, where she received a bachelor of science degree in education, with a minor in art history, and a master of science in education. Recently retired from a career as a reading teacher at Pagosa Springs [Colorado] Junior High, she is at last able to devote herself to sharing her lifelong love of quilts with others.

Other AQS Books

This is only a small selection of the books available from the American Quilter's Society. AQS books are known worldwide for timely topics, clear writing, beautiful color photos, and accurate illustrations and patterns. The following books are available from your local bookseller, quilt shop, or public library.

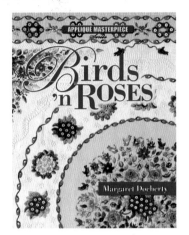

#7013   us$24.95

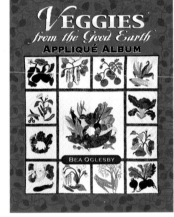

#7017   us$21.95

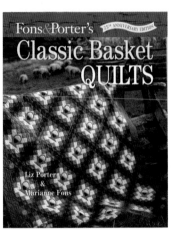

#7011   us$22.95

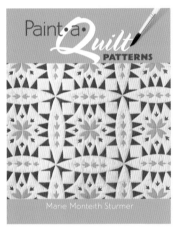

#7016   us$22.95

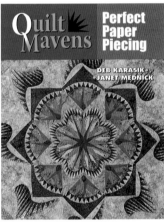

#7018   us$24.95

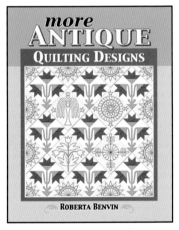

#6907   us$21.95

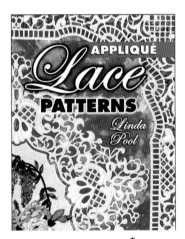

#6906   us$24.95

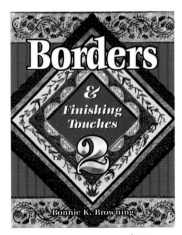

#6804   us$22.95

#6903   us$19.95

Look for these books nationally.
Call or Visit our Web site at

1-800-626-5420
www.AmericanQuilter.com